Language and Reading among Underachievers

Language and Reading among Underachievers:

a practical review

Caroline and David Moseley

NFER Publishing Company Ltd.

Published by the NFER Publishing Company Ltd.,
Darville House, 2 Oxford Road East,
Windsor, Berks. SL4 1DF
Registered Office: The Mere, Upton Park, Slough, Berks. SL1 2D
First published 1977
© National Foundation for Educational Research in England and Wales, 1977
ISBN 0 85633 136 8

Printed in Great Britain by
John Gardner (Printers) Ltd., Hawthorne Road, Bootle, Merseyside L20 6JX.
Distributed in the USA by Humanities Press Inc.,
Atlantic Highlands, New Jersey 07716 USA.

Contents

PREFACE

There are so many titles relevant to our subject that merely to list them, let alone summarize the work, would have taken more than the limited number of words imposed. So instead of a photographic survey we have produced a pen and ink impression of the field. While necessarily subjective, such a study establishes, we hope, the position of important research findings in relation to each other and to the schools, teachers and pupils with which they are concerned.

In the references it has not been possible to include all the work we have read before reaching conclusions. Some large surveys have not yielded original results, while certain studies or small samples are interesting but too unreliable to quote. In other cases findings have been duplicated and here we quote larger-scale work only. The titles given should be enough to introduce readers to the academic literature of more specialist aspects of reading and language development on which most of the arguments are based.

ACKNOWLEDGEMENTS

This work is the result of contributions from many quarters. Beulah Matthews and Eunice Hulford deciphered and typed the manuscript both before and after Denis Vincent, Gill Pugh, Gabriel Chanan, Peter Davies and June Derrick made useful suggestions. Mr A. Gwilliam and the NFER Information Services were consistently successful in their search for obscure articles and rare books. Phil Clift kept us going with his unfailing support and encouragement, and, most important of all, Margaret Thorpe kept the babies happy while we tussled with so-called higher things.

Caroline and David Moseley London 1977

Chapter 1
Points of View

Summary

Interpretation of research often reflects personal and political inclinations. In the field of language and reading development there are many questions that have not been resolved to everybody's satisfaction. After studying the evidence in the light of experience our position on some of these emerges as follows:

It is impossible to conclude that standards of language and reading have either risen or fallen. What is more to the point is that they are generally unnecessarily low; and that there is in some cases conflict between the skills fostered by teachers of English and those expected by other specialist colleagues and employers. Improvement in these two areas is likely to involve schools becoming more accountable to the community at large.

Children differ in their constitutional ability although environment plays a major part in determining their attainment levels.

Many children need explicit language training. This supplements rather than conflicts with the value of free talk.

Group size is the critical determinant of teaching style. Many classes are of the size where teachers cannot effectively use widely approved styles.

Diagnostic testing is only useful as part of a teaching programme. This should be based on individual learning difficulties. Psychologists can play a most effective part in such programmes when they work closely with teachers. There are however, many occasions when the aims of teacher and therapist are different. The psychoanalytic tradition has very little to offer the teacher other than a sense of understanding which in most cases has no perceptible effect on the children themselves.

There is no mystique about good teaching of low achievers. It demands sensitivity to the pupils and their situations, knowledge of methods and materials available, energy and a lot of hard work. These attributes are not easily measured. Thus research findings do not take account of them and are therefore unconvincing to practitioners. Nonetheless many studies can make a useful contribution and it is important to use effective ways of disseminating and adapting their findings.

i. Interpreting research in the behavioural sciences

Legend has it that Alexander the Great was one of the earliest investigators of language development. Determined to establish whether Greek or Hebrew was the natural language of man he ordered ten babies to be reared away from any sound of human speech. Unfortunately none lived to tell the tale. His research seems to have been applied in two ways: positively, in that the impracticality of pure behavioural research is widely recognized; negatively, in that research into language development is still often seen as a weapon in political issues not very closely related to the well-being of the children. The complexity of a normal human environment is only one factor which makes behavioural research conclusions suspect. There are also the personal and political inclinations of the researcher.

The best studies present minutely-detailed objective observations and link every aspect of observed behaviour into a coherent theory. Unfortunately human perception is such that, where something fails to fit a pet hypothesis, we tend not to notice it has happened or not to give it the significance it deserves. In our particular field statistical methods or unreliable tests are mercilessly attacked by academics who disagree with conclusions based on them; similar, or even less objective methods, pass unnoticed in studies that support a sympathetic model.

This is a tendency from which we are unlikely to be immune. Thousands of articles and books are referenced as relevant to reading and language skill in low achievers. We have read as widely and as objectively as we could but our approach was necessarily tempered by classroom experience. This had led us to dismiss certain theoretical positions as untenable. It has sometimes been the deciding factor on the standpoint taken over a major issue.

Much-publicized debate is still raging round certain aspects of language and reading in school. It is an area in which statistical and testing techniques are unlikely to be completely reliable. Because of this, arguments over the validity of certain studies can be relevant but incomprehensible to most educationists. We have checked the research methods used in work subsequently referred to and found them acceptable. But because impartiality is rarely, if ever, achieved, we begin by examining findings on some fundamental issues and by declaring the position we hold from reading the evidence in the light of experience.

ii. Acceptable standards of language and reading

The English language is likely to have been affected by at least two recent developments. Firstly, a move to question authority is linguistically reflected in the debate as to whether any one variant of spoken English should be regarded as standard and taught as such. Secondly, improvements in radio and electronic communications have eradicated the need for accurate and easily understood reading and writing in many situations. It would be surprising if general usage had not changed (some would say deteriorated) to take account of these social changes.

Individuals who cannot use English effectively orally and in writing, are disadvantaged, both individually and in the part they can play in creating a workable democracy. The education system is traditionally responsible for ensuring that children learn to understand, speak, read and write. During 30 years in which social barriers seem to have become less rigid, communication media more widespread and investment in education has been high, it is disappointing to find that no improvement has been measured in the standards achieved by the schools.[1] In present conditions we find convincing evidence that all but severely subnormal school children are capable of learning to read.[2] This means that the influence of school can and should at least partially outweigh the debilitating effects of unfavourable social conditions on literacy. The question, then, is not whether standards have risen or fallen, but why they are not higher.[3]

The next question is more complex and should perhaps have come first. What sort of English should the schools teach? There is a small but influential body of opinion which is constantly stressing the importance of English for self-expression rather than communication.[4] They seem immune to cries from employers and universities bemoaning the impression that school-leavers are not equipped with the language skills necessary to function in the world at large.

It is possibly a coincidence that this voice seems to come mainly from secondary school English specialists whose previous depth studies are likely to have been in English literature. Looking at books which stress the teaching of these personal and imaginative aspects of language[5] one becomes aware that many of the authors are influential members of the National Association for the Teaching of English (NATE). The emphasis within NATE contrasts with that of the National Association for Remedial Education (NARE) or the United Kingdom Reading Association (UKRA), organizations whose members are language teachers of a more general kind.[6]

We do not decry the teaching of expressive and poetic language. We appreciate that personal involvement is necessary to any worthwhile language work and that the NATE lobby has played an important part in fighting useless mechanical English teaching. But we cannot accept the low priority it gives to the teaching of generally accepted rules of communication like spelling and punctuation.[7] Small-scale surveys among parents reveal similar concern on this point.[8] If a pupil's learning of his native language in school does not foster the skills aspired to at home and demanded at work, his position becomes very difficult.

Since standards of acceptable English are established by usage within the community, we suggest that in this area above all others, contact between teachers, parents and employers is vital. A project in Chicago that has achieved such cooperation[9] gives valuable evidence of its possible rewards. The Chicago experience suggests that it is not difficult to agree which varieties of language most benefit the children. Once each group understands what the other is frightened of, there is no need to adopt polarized positions. It would be a relief to see the end of the irrational defences of poetry as opposed to punctuation or vice versa which too often end discussions of how best to ensure easy communication.

iii. The nature/nurture arguments

Studies of identical twins, some pairs reared together, others with the environment of one twin contrasting with that of the other, offer the most widely-accepted method by which the balance between innate ability and environment can be assessed. However the data on which the classic studies are based have lately been convincingly questioned.[10] In Chapter 5 we accept the importance of environmental factors in determining language and reading levels, but even if one denies the influence of genes on intelligence, there is strong evidence that children are not born equal.

Studies of language acquisition have shown great differences between individual children's rates of learning to talk, though their homes seem well-matched, particularly in mother/child interaction.[11] These differences persist and seem to play a part in later school performance.

Many researchers have noted these innate tendencies and tried to explain them.[12] But there is no established reason why some babies seem content to let the world go by, while others delight in finding problems and solving them. The general idea of individual levels of 'equilibrium'—a state of mental restfulness where unsolved problems cease to generate any action—is likely to prove relevant in explaining why some are intellectually insatiable and others placid to the point of lethargy.

When a child reaches school and his language is inadequate it is impossible to tell for some time whether his constitution or his background is the limiting factor. We therefore suggest (section vi, following) that while accepting the existence of innate differences, teaching programmes should be devised to cope with symptoms that can currently be observed and remedied.

On ethnic differences in ability it is impossible to regard the evidence impartially. Jensen's findings of different patterns of abilities between members of different races cannot be demolished.[13] His recommendations for different types of education are not so convincing. It is likely that long-established cultural and social norms will persist in affecting learning even when they have no measurable effects on other aspects of life.

Arguments about the relationship between innate and environmentally conditioned abilities are probably more important politically than educationally. This is reflected in Kamin's attack on Burt.[10] Kamin maintains that Burt emphasized the importance of heredity in order to justify the existence of an élitist education system. In practical terms the issue rarely seems to be as simple as this.

iv. The role of the teacher

In his belief that human beings have a natural tendency to develop language, Chomsky, an American linguist, has spilled a good deal of bile on colleagues who attempt explicitly to teach children how to use their mother-tongue.[14] This might be confusing to inexperienced teachers since Chomsky implies that forceful intervention in the learning process can only be destructive. Of course any teaching method can be misinterpreted and abused. Teaching anybody what to think and what to say in every situation would be a destructive and, we trust, useless exercise. But that is not the point.

To counter Chomsky's negative influence we will outline some accounts of profitable teacher intervention, but first we turn once more to the studies of language acquisition. Brown[11] found no evidence that babies could learn anything without a model. When a child says 'taked' instead of 'took' he is basing his past tense form on the model of most words he hears. When he says 'car-bird' for 'aeroplane' he is combining two ideas he has learned from models.[15] Skinner goes further than this.[16] He contends there are rules which govern whole responses. Although such rules are extremely complex and have not so far been adequately described, further evidence of their likely existence has recently been produced by McLeish.[17]

The mother or her substitute obviously provides the baby's most important learning model. But where the mother can give the child little time, or has herself only partially mastered certain aspects of language (see Chapter 2, section iv), school and teacher have a responsibility to provide the experience the child needs. This will not replicate interaction with a good mother, for the situation is likely to be different in important ways. The child is older which means both that he is more mature and that the programme has less time to bring him to the level of his more able contemporaries; he is also unlikely to find himself in any, let alone 24-hour, daily individual contact with the same concerned adult. These differences alone would indicate the need for a programme which consciously structures and explicitly presents language, necessarily incorporating some intensive group teaching and practice.

Such programmes have been devised, and have been shown to improve children's learning potential. The fact that in general their benefits do not last for ever does not disprove their effectiveness. No other short course is expected to counter-balance for life the long-term future effects of 18 hours of unstimulating surroundings every day.[18] It is therefore surprising that gains ever persist, which they do, and every new study makes it increasingly difficult to deny the benefits of intensive work plus a considerable element of teacher direction.[19]

As children grow up, the language they know and the language they need obviously become much harder to define. We have read often of the need for the teacher to understand, accept and encourage the child to use the language he already knows and uses.[20] This is certainly important, for the involvement and confidence it begets will play a part in determining success in many situations. But these qualities will not in themselves lead to mastery of aspects of language which open the door to some of the easier and pleasanter sides of life. The London Educational Priority Area Team decided to concentrate entirely on the 'confidence' factor in language and set up a programme consisting of a series of outings for a group of children and their parents.[21] Everybody came, and talked, and got on well with the teachers and team members. When the final interviews were held, all were convinced that much had been achieved. But on all objective measures the control group, who had stayed in school, had done slightly better, and at much less cost.

If further proof is needed of the value of explicit teaching, we would mention Mrs Pyrah.[22] Here is a teacher totally committed to widening the children's horizons. While her direction of each new group of children is obvious, by the end of one term each child is beginning to go his own way—and anybody who meets these children before and after her influence can only recognize the positive contribution it makes to their lives.

v. The importance of group size

There are no conclusive studies of the relationship between the size of a teaching group and the achievement of the pupils. Smaller teaching groups tend to consist of children selected because they need some kind of special help, and are therefore not comparable with ordinary large classes. The study we want to emphasize in this section investigates the importance of group size in determining teaching methods.

Olson's team researched 18,528 classrooms.[23] Having asked a most impressive list of educators to isolate the factors they considered most significant in determining educational quality, Olson analysed the replies and found they could be grouped under four headings: individualization, interpersonal regard, group activity and creativity. These he calls the indicators of quality. Intellectual achievement does not feature in its own right. He then identified teaching styles: teacher lecture, teacher questioning and so on. From the observers' findings it was possible to check how the various teaching styles scored on the indicators of quality. It was here that he began to look at the relevance of class size. His findings reveal critical points which indicate that the size of class is a key determinant of teaching style. In primary classes with 25 pupils or fewer, all teachers achieved above-average marks for quality. There were also dramatic score improvements if classes were smaller than 15 and again when there were five pupils or fewer; at secondary level the critical number emerged as 15. When groups grew larger than this the percentage of time the teacher spent lecturing, questioning or setting desk work seemed automatically to rise and 'quality' scores correspondingly dropped. We will be referring to Olson again when we consider economic allocation of teacher time (Chapter 6, section iii).

The relevance of the research is obvious, but there is one implication that we want to underline. In debate about methods of teaching language and reading it is sometimes assumed that teaching style only indicates the attitude of the teacher to his class. The teacher who is authoritarian by nature will lecture while the more radical teacher will let his class talk in groups. Olson's findings force a more detailed exploration of the effect of class size. Perhaps teachers resort to lecturing in big classes because they cannot effectively use the styles they really like. In our experience group work in large secondary classes needs organizational methods and materials that teachers are rarely trained or allowed to use. Otherwise attempts at group work can end up with children copying from library books. Olson found that experimental work in science scored exceptionally high on his quality indicators and suggests it offers a model that might be successfully adapted to other areas of the curriculum. Meanwhile there is obviously good evidence to support the case for smaller teaching groups.

vi. The diagnosis of specific learning disabilities and the part the psychologist can play in effective remedial provision

Common sense (reinforced by the Bullock Report) tells us that there is no point in using sophisticated diagnostic procedures if there is no pay-off in terms of the subsequent action taken. Why obtain a detailed profile of strengths and weaknesses *if* a global teaching programme is just as effective as one with specific objectives?[24] Why ask for medical diagnosis of dyslexia or minimal brain damage *if* there are no clear-cut educational consequences?[25] Why ask for psychiatric opinion about the supposed internal dynamics which may affect a child's ability to learn *if* traditional psychotherapeutic methods have no positive effect on educational performance?[26]

Although there are many research studies which bear on these issues, different and opposing opinions are held, especially among those professionally committed to certain ways of working. We would state our views as follows.

Very little is known about the value of diagnostic assessment and teaching. Remedial teaching in itself does bring immediate benefit, although follow-up studies are disappointing.[27] We don't know exactly why remedial teaching works, but we have reason to believe that it is something to do with a sense of being valued and gaining confidence.[28] Different ways of organizing special educational provision are employed in different parts of the country and in different schools,[29] but we cannot find any experimental evidence which would lead us to recommend a 'best buy'. Our impression is that, with present resources, a lot more could be done to individualize programmes of remedial and special education. Individualized programmes which are carried through with rigour and precision are rare.

It is probable that the proportion of children needing such help is no more than one-third of all those with learning difficulties. However, we feel that it makes better sense to try to improve and to validate present methods than to abandon the idea of diagnostic assessment and teaching.

There is a growing body of evidence for the existence of three or four basic patterns of learning difficulty,[30] but in the majority of cases the surface symptoms have no evident connection with presumed underlying causes, such as genetic factors, developmental lag, minimal brain damage. In our present state of knowledge it is better to plan a remedial programme on the basis of presenting symptoms and behaviour than to apply labels which imply a specific medical condition. The educational term 'learning difficulty' is more satisfactory[31] especially if its meaning is explained to parents and to teachers as it applies to a particular child.

Our reading of the research findings relating to the application of certain psychotherapeutic (Freudian, Jungian, Kleinian) ideas in an educational context is that these ideas lead to no improvement in pupil behaviour or learning. A few examples of positive results (as well as some positively negative findings) are to be found in the literature, but the vast majority of studies are unconvincing and subjective. This is not to deny that some teachers feel enriched and supported through their contact with clinical services, but that is hardly an argument for what many other teachers experience as an inefficient inward-looking system.[32] It is our opinion that LEAs would do well to re-model their child guidance and schools' psychological services in order to respond more efficiently to the behaviour and learning problems which occur in schools and in the community. The literature on behaviour-modification gives us reason to be optimistic here,[33] and this approach lends itself to implementation by teachers and by parents as well as by clinic personnel.

vii. Research and its relevance to the classroom

The need for some knowledge of statistics in evaluating research has already been mentioned. It is also true that many useful research findings are presented in learned journals and intended for highly academic readers. Statistical and experimental methods must be expounded somewhere if findings are to be taken seriously, but busy teachers need easier access if they are to gain early benefit. Research reviews offer a solution to this situation.[34]

But there are likely to be more fundamental reasons for teachers' reputed antipathy to research.[35] For example, nobody has yet managed scientific analysis of what makes a good teacher. We return to this theme in Chapter 4. When methods are evaluated the teacher is likely to be the vital variable[36] and yet so often it is just assumed that teacher strengths were more or less matched. Anybody working in a classroom knows that factors such as a teacher's eye contact, his hesitations, speed of delivery, even his appearance will affect pupils' interest in what he has to offer. The importance of some of these traits has been established in research among social psychologists.[37] Moreover a good teacher will automatically fill in the gaps in bad material or supplement one method with another. For him it is unimportant to supply a foolproof programme, although even that will fail when badly supervised.[38] When Bennett concludes that structured methods generally result in better attainments than unstructured,[39] he offers insights that are useful to those concerned with education at a general level. To the individual teacher, hard-worked, short of resources, the cost of the project seems high and the conclusion, to reflect what he always knew; that it pays to prepare lessons and make sure one thing leads on to another. One can see the temptation to dismiss large-scale general findings and follow intuition rather than spend time following the to-and-fro of the academic debate.

There are two kinds of studies that seem to us particularly important for all practitioners. One, not concerned with evaluation, reports exactly what is going on. It is important for example, to be aware that teachers spend (waste?) a significant part of each day on petty administration;[40] that newly-fledged female teachers discriminate (almost certainly subconsciously) against clever black adolescent boy pupils;[41] that nobody manages to teach phonics in classrooms with a high external noise level, e.g. near a shunting yard or main road.[42]

The second kind of research with immediate practical implications is concerned with details of teaching method. It reports, on film or videotape, exactly what happened on a given occasion; what sort of children were in the class; how the teacher handled not only the subject but also the classroom nuisance. Where a child is working individually with a teacher it shows interaction that cannot be adequately conveyed in print. There are some welcome indications that this is beginning to be recognized.[43] The cost, in money terms, is high. But in case, in these times of economic stringency, anybody thinks audiovisual reporting is unnecessary we end with a warning. A printed transcription of a tape recording, let alone an indirect report, gives a totally inadequate, not to say useless impression of speech. Accent, intonation, pauses are an essential part of spoken language. Researchers have perhaps had to submit to market pressures on the presentation of their findings but readers must accept the very strict limitations of the printed word in analysing and reporting work concerned with the teaching at language and reading in school.

Notes to Chapter 1

1. Investigations are summarized in the Bullock Report (DES, 1975).
2. Ablewhite, 1967; Morgan, 1971.
3. In Chapter 4 findings are quoted which reveal how low achievements are in some schools and areas.
4. Professor Britton sums up their view in his note of extension to the Bullock Report (DES, 1975). To illustrate it we quote an extract from Britton *et al.*, 1975 which begins by quoting from a pupil's work:

   "'It is quite easy to make oxygen if you have the right equipment necessary. You will need a test tube (a large one), a stand with some acid in it. You will need also a Bunsen burner, of course you must not forget a glass tank too. A thin test tube should fix neatly in its place. When you have done that fill the glass tank and put the curve end upwards. Put the glass tank on the table and fill with water. Very soon you will find that you made oxygen and glad of it.'"

   We wondered whether the girl's science teacher was glad she was glad of it. We wondered also whether this was the sort of thing that science teachers were afraid of, the reason why they fought shy of the kind of writing in which a learner directly documents experience as he feels its first impact; not at this stage working upon it to sort out what belongs to the world experienced and what to the individual who experiences. Surely the moment would come when the writer of this piece could learn without difficulty that it is one thing to describe an experiment (for the purpose of repeating it if she wanted to, or for the sake of someone else who wanted to try), and another thing to describe how she felt about it when first she performed it. Meanwhile, her being glad about it, and prepared to say so, augurs well, one might suppose, for the expenditure of such effort as she might need to make her description more accurate, more informative, and so more useful.'

   The authors' comment leaves two important questions unanswered: how is the science teacher to know if the girl has understood how to make oxygen and if she has, who is going to teach her to make the useful report that all parties are likely to want to encourage? Spontaneous and endearing as her 'gladness' is, it might be well founded in relief at finding oxygen when both the crucial part of the experiment and the language for explaining it are far from her grasp.'

5. Britton *et al.*, 1975; Jones and Mulford, 1971; Martin *et al.*, 1976; Rosen and Rosen, 1973; Stratt *et al.*, 1973.
6. An opinion founded on evidence from the journals of the three associations:

   English in Education (NATE)
   Remedial Education (NARE)
   Reading (UKRA).

It might be related to the Bullock finding (DES, 1975) that less able secondary school children are more likely to be taught English by one who is not a qualified English specialist.

7. In only one chapter of the works listed in note 5 is consideration given to the need to teach spelling and punctuation.
8. Lynch and Pimlott, 1976.
9. Stenner and Mueller, 1974.
10. Kamin, 1974.
11. Brown, 1973, presents the most comprehensive summary of the evidence.
12. Hebb, 1955; Hunt, 1961.
13. Jensen, 1969.
14. Chomsky, 1959.
15. Polly Moseley, 1975, unpublished utterances.
16. Skinner, 1957.
17. McLeish and Martin, 1975.
18. A point made by Tizard, 1975.
19. Bereiter and Engelmann, 1966; Blank and Solomon, 1968; Gray and Klaus, 1970; Weikart, 1971.
20. A need emphasized in too many works to list. DES, 1975 and all the books referenced in note 5 serve as examples.
21. Barnes, 1975.
22. Recorded in Moseley, C., 1972. One of the authors spent a great deal of time with this class. It soon became obvious that the slow clear speech the children use in lessons is only to ensure they will be heard. In individual conversation they speak at normal speed. The matter of their conversation is spontaneous and quite disconcertingly perceptive.
23. Olson, 1971.
24. Dumont, 1974.
25. Reed et al., 1968; Scott, 1976.
26. Elliott and Pumfrey, 1972; Morse et al., 1964; Pumfrey and Elliott 1970.
27. Carroll, 1972; Dumont, 1974; Moseley, 1975a.
28. Lawrence and Blagg, 1974.
29. Moseley, 1975a.
30. Mattis et al., 1975; Naidoo, 1972.
31. DES, 1972.
32. Nichol, 1974.
33. Hamblin et al., 1971; Thoresen, 1973; Ward, 1976.
34. For example, Goodacre's reviews in Reading.
35. Gilliland, 1976.
36. Widlake, 1972.
37. Open University, 1972.
38. Lindwall and Bolvin, 1967.
39. Bennett, 1976.
40. Hilsum and Cane, 1971.
41. Rubowits and Maehr, 1973.
42. Cane and Smithers, 1971.
43. Tough, 1976, is published with accompanying videotapes.

Chapter 2
Defining a Language Problem

Summary

There are pitfalls in attempting to assess language ability. Situation is very important in determining performance. Checklists are of particular use and there are also various published tests which can be of value. Certain syntactical aspects of language seem to cause recurrent difficulty and this probably arises for reasons which lie beyond the grammar involved.

1. The difficulty of assessing language ability

The definition of a language problem is a subjective, not to say political, matter. There is now a considerable body of evidence to support the contention that children of working class parents use language less, and less effectively, in school than their middle class counterparts.[1] They also generally score lower on all kinds of formal tests involving vocabulary and language ability, and on measures of intelligence (not surprisingly, in view of the high verbal content of most IQ tests). The evidence is controversial however on two important connected issues: whether this reflects a real difference of language ability or just a difference of performance in a particular setting; and whether it will actually have affected the level of a child's cognition.[2] These questions must be considered when we are trying to establish which children have language problems and what these problems really are.

The concept of *communicative competence* is useful to this discussion. Chomsky first coined the phrase to express the language level at which an individual could function if he were not inhibited by shyness, boredom or any other adverse factors. It is perhaps best described as the language level at which a pupil can operate inside his head, external conditions rarely if ever being favourable enough to permit his actually expressing himself at this level. Since language can only be measured by *performance*, (what is actually said or written), competence cannot be measured, only guessed at.

To illustrate the importance of competence as opposed to performance, let us consider the results of an experiment which, over six months, increased Terry's intelligence score from a quotient of 57 to one of 131[3]. An innately dull child would be unlikely to achieve such a massive gain, and it is not surprising to read in the research report that Terry came from a home where all his efforts to communicate were positively discouraged. His problem can be diagnosed not as a problem of competence but as one of performance. Although all his initial symptoms were those of an ill-adjusted boy of very low ability, his need was primarily for encouragement to speak and to respond, and all the rest followed[4]. Now if Terry had been part of a different project or of no project at all, he could well have been branded as ESN and have progressed or regressed at a rate which would have made the label seem appropriate.

Although the case of Terry is unusually extreme it illustrates the dangers inherent in interpreting scores on so-called language or verbal-reasoning tests. *A low score on a language test is a symptom that something is wrong somewhere rather than proof that a child lacks language skill.* Scores can rise dramatically when the child begins to feel at home with the tester[5] or when he realizes that for once in his life somebody genuinely wants him to talk rather than shut up[3]. So we can confidently suggest that many of the big language/verbal reasoning gains made by disadvantaged children on compensatory education projects, might have little to do with development of their communicative competence. They might reflect merely the child's developing ability to cope with what has been an inhibiting situation for him.

In fairness to the children we cannot over-emphasize the dangers of using language tests in certain situations, for example when the results might be used to classify children in a way which would limit their academic progress in school; or when teachers might accept the results as a predictor of a child's future attainment. (If there is any need to predict progress, the best way to do it is to measure attainment on a common syllabus—a subject beyond the scope of this paper[6].) Instruments for measuring language ability mislead rather than inform, unless they are used as an integral part of diagnostic teaching.

Back to the classroom then, and to a live illustration of what this means in terms of sorting out your 'language problems' at the beginning of the Autumn term. Obviously every classroom makes different language demands but the situation set up for an Open University language course radio programme[7] is typical of a kind. Two different junior school conversations are presented: one among a group of lecturers' children (group A), the other among car-workers' children (group B). Both groups are discussing pets at the instigation of their teacher. The presenter's commentary isolates linguistic features which distinguish the groups—group A for example uses long sentences, plenty of adjectives, group B's utterances are shorter, hesitations longer, and so on.

If you erase the commentary and listen to the speech samples, you might notice other differences. The first group's pets all flourished, grew spots and fins, and had puppies, while poor old B's pets mostly died, were put to sleep, got sent away. Now there is no denying that on almost any measure you might apply in this situation, the group B children will score lower. They have missed out on a good deal of useful background to this exercise. They seem more inhibited by the teacher's presence than the lecturers' children do; they have probably never been allowed to keep up a flow of prattle for its own sake. Moreover the loquacious children have had rich, varied and happy experience of the subject 'pets'. They have handled their fauna under careful supervision, and been rewarded both by people and events for taking a close interest in all that happened to them. Not surprisingly, they handle the subject well in the abstract medium of speech; they have the knowledge to make appropriate generalizations and categorizations; they approach this area of life with optimistic confidence, and nobody who hears them briefly is likely to conclude that these are tomorrow's rulers (a reaction which is in itself likely to encourage them to perform well and be favourably assessed).

But the more you listen to the tape the more eloquent become the short utterances and long hesitations of some of the group B children. One of the more sensible—realizing he's hopelessly lacking in the right sort of real experience—decides to do something about it. He has the bright idea of talking about his pet chimpanzee. His contribution seems more related to fantasy than fact and is received with little encouragement from the teacher.

Group B are obviously disadvantaged in this particular game; but before making any finite generalizations about their language ability let us try a different set of rules. Labov[8] gives us one idea of how this might be done. He goes into school with a white rabbit called Vincent tucked under his coat and explains to a class of five-year-olds that Vincent is 'kind of nervous'. If someone will talk to the rabbit he'll settle down. Of course everyone volunteers. Harold, James and Mays ('the least verbal child in the class' and two of his pals) are chosen and accompany Labov and Vincent to a room where a tape recorder is set up. The researcher disappears, the tape recorder goes on turning and the children get to work on the rabbit. They produce complex sentences, hypothetical clauses, logical narrative, etc., etc . . .

There are other accounts of ways in which adults have managed to get a clearer idea of how so-called disadvantaged children handle language under conditions that suit them (i.e. begin to get near expression of their communicative competence)[9]. In this type of work assessment and remediation are inseparable. Experience suggests that once a child knows that a teacher knows how well he can talk, that child will continue to perform at a surprisingly high level until he changes teachers[10].

The first step therefore in any assessment of language is to make sure that the communication barrier has been well and truly broken down, that the child is in a situation with which he is confidently familiar. Then and only then can any of the more established measures of language be used with any degree of accuracy. It is to these much-abused-because-wrongly-used measures that we will now turn.

ii. Means of assessing language

In primary school *teachers' checklists* are a justly popular means of focussing attention on each child and isolating those who might need special help. They have the great advantage of recording language behaviour in everyday classroom situations. Many schools and individual teachers will have evolved their own lists; others have been drawn up for wider use by teams from national projects and local authorities.[11] The Communication Skills in Early Childhood project has emphasized the value of a checklist.[12] However it must be clearly established exactly what is being recorded and why. As a teacher education device, a list will make teachers listen more to their pupils, but as a record of progress its value is extremely limited. This is obvious in the light of the fact that no categories of language, no order of development and no order of importance in a hierarchy of skills have ever been agreed. In fact theorists have tended to produce each his own personal terms for the aspects of language he considers distinct and important.[13] A checklist can therefore have no general validity and is unlikely to include all fundamental language skills.

As a measure and for record purposes, therefore, the checklist can only isolate symptoms connected with performance in a particular situation. The children who show up as needing extra help should be those who, on close observation such as that recommended by Dr Tough,[12] are malfunctioning in the classroom. Once pinpointed they will need confidence-building activities—opportunities to talk in less formal situations, or about familiar objects for example. Such work may in itself solve the problem. If language weaknesses persist when the teacher or psychologist has satisfied himself that there can be no emotional reason for them, the checklist has served its purpose and it is time for more formal testing.

It is important that any list used for screening or record purposes should be short enough to allow a class teacher to observe the behaviour of each individual against each item. If a single mark is based on impression rather than observation the validity of the exercise is ruined. We therefore suggest a list of not more than six items. When the lists are only designed for internal use, items should be based on the pupils' likely weaknesses in conjunction, particularly at secondary level, with the language demands made by the individual school or classroom. Pupils' age, geographical and socioeconomic environment, school language policy and individual teachers' methods are among the conditions that are likely to affect both.

As our work is necessarily general, we will examine the areas which researchers have identified as symptomatic of language disadvantage in school children aged eight or under. These are the children who, like Terry, often withdraw, distract or are distracted whenever they are asked to listen. They look blank when they are asked to do anything, often trying to see what the others are doing instead of listening hard to see what is being asked. They very rarely initiate conversations with either a question or an observation. When asked to carry a message they are either tongue-tied or produce garble. If they do talk spontaneously they will utter single words or short sentences. Now all these symptoms could well arise from a multitude of causes. Two pupils could obtain identical screening scores: one is quite unused to, and inhibited by, teacher-like adults; the other doesn't speak a word of English.

No checklist could adequately discriminate in every case. For screening purposes at the beginning of a teaching programme we suggest the following items are fundamental. As soon as they have been checked we would press for teacher action to be modified along the lines indicated to take account of certain scoring patterns:

1. Listens with interest	(a) to other children	never sometimes often
	(b) to the teacher	never sometimes often
2. Obviously understands instructions	(a) from other children	never sometimes often
	(b) from the teacher	never sometimes often
3. Asks questions	(a) of other children	never sometimes often
	(b) of the teacher	never sometimes often
4. Volunteers information	(a) to other children	never sometimes often
	(b) to the teacher	never sometimes often
5. Carries messages successfully	(a) between children and teacher	never sometimes
	(b) from one child to another	never sometimes

Scoring

1. Any child with five or more 'nevers' should be visited at home by the teacher so the teacher can ascertain whether the parents speak English or whether there is any other particularly inhibiting factor in the child's background.
2. Any child with three or four 'nevers' is likely to need more confidence in the classroom before his language ability can be usefully assessed.
3. Any child not in categories 1 or 2 (i.e. scoring 'never' twice or less)

but *not* scoring '*often*' more than five times might usefully be tested (by his own familiar teacher) on a more formal measure.

The most important feature of any of the following *tests* is that they should be given by somebody the pupil likes and chats with. There is evidence that black children in New York achieve about the same as white children when tested by computer, but significantly less well when tested by a person.[14] The harmful effect of the Wrong Tester on a language test score cannot be over-emphasized.

The English Picture Vocabulary Test[15] is the only test of receptive vocabulary widely standardized (for four different age ranges) in this country. It is a test of silent vocabulary comprehension in that the tester says a word, the child looks at four pictures and points to the one that represents the item. (In the group version the child rings the appropriate number or picture.) The fact of not asking for a verbal response is meant to overcome shyness. However experiments have shown that low-scoring children make gains when a second test is administered a week later.[5] This suggests there is a confidence/familiarity factor. The test does not diagnose particular areas of weakness. These two characteristics limit its usefulness either as a pre- and post-test measure of learning or as a diagnostic measure which could be of use to teachers planning individual work.

The Boehm Test of Basic Concepts[16] is much more closely related to the words essential to classroom functioning. It was standardized on a big population of five- to seven-year-olds in the States. In it, children are asked to recognize (and in the group version, ring) pictures representing concepts of space, time, quantity and so on, selected as particularly significant items in various comprehension tests. 'At the top', 'next', 'through' will serve as examples of the concepts. They are well contextualized. One of the main advantages of this test is the part it plays in teacher education. When teachers realize that some of their pupils really don't understand these words they will often begin to teach them systematically. Anybody intending to use this or the following test should eliminate one or two Americanisms that would confuse British children. These do not invalidate the underlying usefulness of either test.

The Assessment of Children's Language Comprehension (ACLC)[17] can also add to a teacher's insight. This has been provisionally standardized for children between three and six-and-a-half years old. It is the only test we have found designed to show how many elements of language a child can process. In the first section of the test the tester says just one word, and the child selects the appropriate picture; then two elements are combined, e.g. 'a *dog eating*'; then three elements, 'a *bus under* a *bridge*'; and then four. The distracting pictures ensure that the child must retain and process all the elements to get the right answer. This test draws attention to a neglected feature of language disability. Several children who may be brain damaged or who may have had little practice in listening, need specific training to increase their comprehension span even though all the actual words are well within their grasp.

The listening unit of Concept 7–9[18] touches on this area and the child's ability to cope with the exercises can tell the teacher a lot. As its name implies, this material is intended for seven- to nine-year-olds, and anybody intending to use it with younger children or children who perform badly, can very profitably record sequences of supplementary items at the lower levels.

The most thoroughly researched measure of language is the Illinois Test of Psycholinguistic Abilities (ITPA).[19] It adds up to a close approximation to verbal intelligence scales. Children with reading problems and disadvantaged children with language problems show typical patterns of deficit which can be remedied by structured educational programmes placing special emphasis on the relevant skills.[20] Karnes[21] has produced ITPA-based courses of language development which are intended for groups of five to eight children in school or for individual use at school or in the home. While it cannot be claimed that this material is a statistically or even theoretically sound set of precision instruments,[22] the thinking behind ITPA does bring with it a welcome change of emphasis. For the reading teacher, the importance of breaking down complex material into chunks that can be 'held' mentally pending a search for meaning or further clues to meaning is highlighted.[23] Awareness of both the sound and grammatic structure of spoken language is emphasized in both language development and in early reading[24] and the value of structured methods in increasing the child's ability to form associations and concepts has now been well established in controlled experiments.[25]

The twelve sub-tests which make up the ITPA are not sufficiently reliable to be used singly. Some of them (e.g. the analogies and digit repetition tests) are traditional in format, while others have novel features. Some LEAs are producing test batteries of their own, often based on some of the ITPA ideas. This involves a major effort of test construction, which will be worthwhile if greater reliability can be achieved, and if the assessment tools are put in the hands of teachers. The ITPA itself is not available to teachers in this country (against the wishes of its originators), nor are there any training courses for teachers who want to use the test. An unfortunate result of this is that teachers are only slowly coming to understand the importance of sequencing and closure skills. In terms of language and reading, sequencing means the ability to remember and to order a series of 'chunks', and closure refers to their integration into meaningful or grammatically well-formed wholes.

The Picture Language Scale[26] is a test of expression which, although originally devised for pre-school children has proved quite hard enough for inner city infants.[27] It is a crude measure, but its strength lies in the fact that the child names objects grouped by subject areas, four tools, four vehicles, and so on. The results help a teacher to know where a child has had plenty of experience and where he lacks it. Many teachers have objected to the pictures, but trials have shown that if a child does not respond to the picture he is equally stumped by the real object.[28] It is interesting to note the number of times a child knows the function of an object but cannot think of its name (e.g. looks at the broom and says 'You sweep with it', but when asked 'And what do you call it?' cannot think of the word). This implies that a child's experience is adequate but he needs help in summoning his words quickly and to order.

Tests which attempt to measure the complexity of language a child can produce are too dependent on situation to be satisfactory, as we saw earlier in this chapter. Informal tape recording probably offers the most hopeful results even in the case of immigrant children who were brought up to speak a language other than English. The tapes should be transcribed so that the teacher can see both what the child wants to say and what he is able to say in a given situation. He is then in a good position to help the pupil to say what he wants. More formal tests of expression are part of the NFER proficiency tests, a special battery devised to measure progress among non-English speakers.[29] The marking matrix from these tests can be adapted and applied to the freer recording mentioned above. However the battery as a whole has two basic limitations. Firstly no account is taken of language *function*. This means that complex language scores high even where short simple sentences are more effective. Secondly, teachers working with non-English speakers would often like some way of comparing their pupils' language with that of English children of the same age, and as yet it has not been possible to even approach the problems of norms of expression for native speakers.[30]

These considerations lead us directly to the difficulties of diagnosing language problems among older children. There is general agreement that a child will be able to understand and use more common structures of English by the age of six.[31] There are about 500 English words which are used with much greater frequency than any others,[32] and these too are likely to be within his grasp. However, development from this core will be an individual matter. Which words a child will 'know', and which he will need to cope with classroom demands, are questions which are just beginning to be answered in general terms.

Since children inevitably spend a large proportion of their time listening to the teacher and to group discussion, it makes sense to treat the teaching and assessment of more advanced listening skills as fundamental. Good listening obviously involves far more than factual recall of details. It is of value both in its own right and as a model for the large variety of remembering and thinking skills that are expected to enter into any kind of understanding and learning. A test of listening comprehension which can give the teacher a good idea of the linguistic competence of her class, and of the kinds of questions she would be asking them is therefore extremely welcome. It can also help to define objectives for backward readers, since the remedial teacher would hope to be able to build up reading skills to the point where further progress in reading becomes dependent on general language development. Where British and American instruments in this field have not so far met the standards that one looks for in objective tests, the New Zealand Council for Educational Research[33] have done better. Their listening comprehension tests are the result of an exemplary exercise in test development and they are probably a great deal more suitable for use in this country than the average American test. They consist of a series of short passages read by the teacher, followed by orally presented questions in multiple choice form. The age range is seven to 15 years, and there are two equivalent forms. The practice of using the tests in conjunction with the NFER Reading Comprehension tests[34] has much to commend it as it gives an indication as to whether pupils' reading limitations arise primarily from vocabulary or mechanical difficulties. It is to be hoped that a publisher will soon decide to make the test available in the UK.

iii. The need to simplify teacher language

When researchers look at classroom language they nearly always end up emphasizing how the behaviour of the individual teacher is most important in reaching a valid estimate of what the children can do. Teachers tend to listen too little and talk too much,[35] often unaware of their own cultural and academic assumptions. To make teachers aware of these tendencies in themselves is automatically to expose, and thence to ease, the children's difficulties. The pupils are the best masters in this situation. If each child is given a chance to respond in his own way and the teachers are helped to observe these responses, the gap between what the pupils have heard and what they have understood becomes obvious. Perhaps pupils would reveal more of their thought processes if they were actually encouraged to make mistakes.

This is well illustrated in the context of the repetition test—a simple technique of asking the child to repeat a short sentence after the teacher. Although memory plays a part in repetition, it can give important insights into other facets of language comprehension and expression as long as sentences are limited to eight words.[36] Failure to repeat exactly will often take the form of grammatical simplification, but this must be interpreted to mean that the information contained in the sentence in terms of meaning and/or grammar, exceeds the amount that can be processed by the pupil. Where pupils are confronted by longer listening tasks (as they usually are in the classroom) and memory fails, it is justifiable to conclude that they have been overloaded, probably by a combination of the content and form of the language they have been subjected to. To examine this in detail we use the limited context of a test which one of the authors used with a group of 11-year-old children in an ESN school in York.[37] The deviant sentences some of the children produced reflected conclusions of published research in various specific areas.

The children tended to simplify the sentence grammatically to the level at which they felt at home, e.g.

cue sentence: Bill's banging his desk make the teacher cross.
pupil's response: Bill's banging the desk and the teacher's cross.

This simplification usually, as here, revealed that the pupil had more or less understood and digested the information, even if the teacher's 'grammar' was not for him. Thus,

cue sentence: to get all your sums right is hard.
pupil's response: sums is hard.

However where the subject matter of the sentence was unfamiliar or emotive the pupil's response often reflected his own view rather than any attempt to understand the teacher. The word 'sums', for example, proved highly emotive for this group and the overall score on this particular item was specially low. The attempts to repeat this sentence included.

> I can't do sums.
> I don't like sums.
> You can't get all your sums right . . . etc.

A twin sentence identically structured (To cross the road without looking is dangerous) did not produce such complications.

Unfamiliar or unexpected content also upset the pupils. Thus

cue sentence: The Saxons were beaten by the Danes.
most common deviation: The Saxons beat the Danes.

although they proved quite able to cope with passives in more familiar contexts, *viz.*:

cue sentence: Mice are eaten by cats.
most common deviation: Cats eat mice.

Now since most teachers are attempting to extend a pupil's knowledge their subject matter will constantly verge on the unfamiliar and any confusing structures are best avoided. The last example, incorporating the passive voice, leads briefly to the literature examining the constructions which fall into this category. Passives where subject and agent might be reversed (as Saxons and Danes above) are particularly open to misconstruction. Certainly

> The Danes beat the Saxons

seems much easier to grasp than the cue sentence given.

Reid[38] found that seven-year-old children understood written material better when she had eliminated certain syntactic features. Although it is hard to regulate speech in accordance with these findings, textbook writers and teachers preparing recorded or written material would do well to check the article. The 'difficult' points can either be consciously taught or eliminated in individual work assignments. Loban[39] looking at older children's writing, found that ambiguity and real mistakes were often caused, particularly among less able children, by the unclear way they used pronouns to refer to previously mentioned (or not mentioned) words and ideas. These same children,

like Reid's young subjects, often fail to relate the word 'it' or 'he' to the
right object or person in language they read or hear, and their odd
comments occasionally reveal their upside-down idea of what the
teacher thinks he has taught.

On unfamiliar ground, then, any of us are likely to misinterpret
what we are told. More aware of this than most, school children
assiduously avoid any attempt to reproduce new facts in their own
words, for by mastering the form of the teacher's language and
reproducing it exactly, just as a shorthand writer records sounds
without being aware of their meaning, the pupil can too often get by
without exposing his lack of understanding. Occasionally the technique fails. Thus the York children listening to a tape/slide programme, then recording their own commentary to the slides, looked at
a picture of a plough pulled by oxen:

Master-tape: Oxen are sometimes used for ploughing in Europe.
Children's commentary: Oxen are sometimes used for ploughing in
York.

These sort of auditory confusions are the matter of many legendary
howlers. We realize all this is old hat. But on this point the findings of
surveys and random observation are equally depressing.[35] Time and
again teachers genuinely believe that they are helping pupils to learn in
depth, while observers in those very classrooms record lessons consisting largely of teacher-lecture followed by closed questions demanding
mechanical responses. Original comments that do not 'fit in' are
ignored or dismissed.

iv. Language in different social contexts

One cannot leave a discussion of difficulties in school language
without referring to the work of Basil Bernstein. He began by
publishing an important article exploring the link between social class
and educational failure. He concluded that differences in language
were a major cause of the barrier between working class children and
educational success. He coined two now familiar terms: *restricted code*
describes the language of working class children. It is a style which
tacitly assumes that the listener understands the context of the speech.
Thus, for example, in an interview, a restricted code speaker might
refer to people without explaining who they are, or to a place like 'the
factory' or the 'den' without explaining its significance. *Elaborated
code* describes a style which fills in the full context of an account. It is

therefore language which needs no particular context and does not assume that the listener is a member of the speaker's own particular class or culture group.

Unfortunately Bernstein went beyond this definition and listed grammatical features that characterized the two codes. Since then he has published and edited a series of writings expounding and modifying his original theory.[40] Constant restatement has left some confusion over the exact nature of his analysis of class differences in language.

His own research team, among others,[41] soon found that the differences went beyond grammar. Children of all backgrounds proved equally able to use and understand English structure given the right situation. The linguists meanwhile were continuing their explorations into different styles of speech (which are technically called 'codes'). They suggest that children from less favoured backgrounds have little experience of the more formal codes that they are likely to meet in the classroom.[42] This could have exactly the effect that Bernstein had observed. Pupils would be puzzled and possibly alienated by teacher talk, while the teacher might interpret short answers as either rude or stupid.

Bernstein is among those who think that the baby's relationship with his mother is important in determining later intellectual achievement. Much of the research has not established just where the link lies and we suggest it has concentrated on how words are strung together instead of looking at the words themselves and the richness of meaning they are likely to convey to children from different backgrounds.[43] To children from less articulate homes the words will be familiar but will not have their full connotation. To these children school language might seem like a poem full of classical allusions would seem to those of us who have not had a classical education. We recognize the names and feel we should know the story behind them, but strive in vain to grasp their implications.

To illustrate the situation in reverse we retell one of our favourite stories; that of the London probationer starting her teaching career in Somerset. Choosing a subject to suit her class she pins up a picture of a cow.

'What's that?' she says.

Silence

'Surely you've all noticed those in the fields. Why there are some at the back of the school. What's this then?'

After a long pause a hand is slowly put up.

'I think, Miss, it could be a two-year-old short-horn heifer.'

Notes to Chapter 2

1. For example, Davie *et al.*, 1972; Halsey, 1972.
2. The link between language and cognition is far from established. Findings imply that perception improves with vocabulary.
3. Hamblin *et al.*, 1971.
4. Details of the programme are given in Chapter 3 of Hamblin above. It began with food reinforcement and continued on a fairly strict behaviourist model, with rewards when Terry talked, answered questions, mixed sociably with other children, and so on.
5. Zigler *et al.*, 1973.
6. Of course most tests and exams are of this kind. An account of devising a pure example is given in Haynes, 1971.
7. Lee, 1972.
8. Labov, 1970.
9. Labov, 1969; Strandbery and Griffiths, quoted in Cazden, 1970.
10. Moseley, 1972.
11. Wolfendale and Bryans, 1972.
12. Tough, 1976.
13. For example, Britton, 1970; Moffett, 1968; examples quoted by Pearce in Doughty *et al.*, 1972.
14. Johnson and Mihal, 1973.
15. Brimer and Dunn, 1962.
16. Boehm, 1967.
17. Foster *et al.*, 1972.
18. Wight *et al.*, 1973.
19. Kirk *et al.*, 1968.
20. Pumfrey, 1975.
21. Karnes, 1968; Karnes, 1972.
22. Waugh, 1975.
23. Hirshoren, 1969; Pumfrey, 1975.
24. Hirshoren, 1969; Karnes, 1972; Pumfrey, 1975.
25. For example, Blank and Solomon, 1968; Jacobson and Greeson, 1972; Karnes *et al.*, 1970.
26. Remedial Supply Co., 1972.
27. A small survey carried out by the author in Haringey in 1972.
28. A.J. Evans, 1972.
29. NFER, 1973.
30. We have already mentioned the lack of a generally agreed way of classifying language or imposing a developmental order beyond the earliest stages of acquisition. Some differing attempts are referenced in note 13.
31. Reiterated by Brown, 1973.
32. Edwards and Gibbon, 1964; McNally and Murray, 1962.
33. Elley and Reid, 1971.
34. Barnard, 1976.
35. Barnes *et al.*, 1969; Flanders, 1970; and other interaction studies.

36. Graham, 1968. It was the repetition tests devised for these experiments that were
    adopted for the York survey.
37. Moseley, 1970.
38. Reid, 1972.
39. Loban, 1966.
40. Bernstein, 1971; 1973; 1975.
41. Bernstein, 1973.
42. Pearce in Doughty *et al.*, 1972, explores linguistic analyses in this area.
43. Whorf, 1956.

Chapter 3
The Relationship between Language and Reading Skills

Summary
In the early stages, the language demands of most reading schemes are well within the grasp of all normal children from English-speaking homes. At reading age eight, however, there is a dramatic increase in the number of words used in books and texts. Pupils' reading comprehension may well be limited by inadequate vocabulary at this stage.

The link between oracy and literacy in more advanced reading is complex. In spite of the prevalence of the theory that oracy precedes literacy, even at this stage research is still exploratory, and no patterns have been established.

i. Language in the early stages of reading
Language and reading interact in different ways at different stages of schooling.

To begin with, teachers might feel that silent five- to seven-year-olds cannot learn to read because they have a 'language problem'. While this is possibly true in the case of non-English speakers, in children of English-speaking parents the problem is likely to be more complex. In a small but carefully controlled experiment[1] quantity rather than quality of language recorded was the indicator of how well the children of working class parents reacted to reading.

This finding is predictable when we examine the language of early reading books. Actual vocabulary or ability to cope with long sentences is unlikely to unlock the door to literature at this stage. A typical reading series[2] designed for first year juniors starts with a book which uses 138 different words grouped in sentences averaging six words in length. These figures should be borne in mind when teachers are examining pre-reading tests and materials. Many[3] include exercises of vocabulary which go way beyond anything an infant school pupil is likely to meet in print. Children who do badly in vocabulary tests (a characteristic which may be related more to confidence than ability, as we find in Chapter 1) are likely to be judged as unready for reading and to suffer accordingly. The research on this subject[4] shows that:

1. Children who have been exposed to detailed pre-reading programmes do not learn to read any quicker than those who have not;
2. Many of the so-called pre-reading skills are not related to reading.

The same arguments do not apply to schemes for teaching patterns of learning behaviour (concentration, taking turns in games, etc.).[5] These habits have to be established, and may need to be taught in very familiar contexts before any specific new skill such as reading can be taught.

Although we can assume that early books do not over-tax the vocabulary or memory of their readers, many of them do not reflect normal speech patterns. This is a serious defect. It stops a child from being able to predict the next word, and prediction plays a part in later reading fluency. It also prevents the reader from accepting the written word as an extension of speech, and again later this will inhibit the children's writing and perhaps make them unwilling to treat the printed word as a relevant, flexible source of information instead of a source of mechanical exercises.

ii. Vocabulary demands of second-stage reading

Between seven and eight children are obviously expected to make a big step forward in their reading. In the series we've already mentioned Book 2 (reading age 7.4 years[6]) has 299 different words where Book 4 (reading age 8.0 years) has 1004.[2] The tests reflect this leap and teachers who use the well-known word recognition tests will remember how steep the grading seems at this point.[7] At six and a half a child is expected to cope with

low   everyone   mischief   friendly   because

while at eight he must decipher

gracious   ocean   quarrelsome   neighbourhood   jealousy

It is interesting that children must *pronounce* the words correctly in order to score. This means that a child who develops his vocabulary largely from the printed word is likely to score much better on silent reading tests than on word recognition.

Herein lies a clue as to why so many children stick at a reading age of around eight. They are beginning to meet words—particularly in reference books—which will not be very familiar. Pupils are now at an advantage if they live in an environment where all kinds of subjects are discussed. In this way the words acquire meaning for the child in relation to his own world. The connotations of a word will be much richer to the child who has heard it used and tried to use it himself in a variety of situations.

There is evidence[8] that children who can cope in concrete situations and relate one 'thing' to another, cannot make the same associations when presented with words. They are likely to be less able to apply verbal information creatively, i.e. to relate it profitably to their own experience. So here we are, back at the children who are able to copy or repeat words but do not understand them enough for them to mean something in terms of their own lives.

Such difficulties are more severe in connection with the printed word than the spoken. Print does not offer any clues to meaning in intonation or gesture, quite apart from sheer mechanical difficulties. Pupils will often be interested in a book that is read aloud, but not bother to go beyond a page or two when left to read it for themselves, although they are quite capable of decoding the words. A reader often mutters sentences to himself when he is trying to absorb difficult information or ideas from a book; the intonation and pauses are an aid to understanding. However some children will never have been exposed to spoken language at this level and cannot therefore avail themselves of the help it offers.

The disadvantages of coming from an inarticulate home increase in relation to reading comprehension as children progress up the school. Students are asked to generalize more[9], an exercise that involves language development and usually means thinking in more abstract terms. Such abstractions are meaningless unless they are constantly measured and modified in the light of each pupil's experience. This is best done in 'experimental' talk with somebody well-informed. Teachers find it difficult to organize work like this in groups bigger than five pupils[10]. It is perhaps relevant to mention that improved reading ages are recorded among students who attend small-group and individual counselling[11]. Maybe the school counsellor is the most stimulating English teacher the children have encountered—or perhaps he is merely favoured by the relative smallness of his group.

There is evidence among young children that structured practice in certain mechanical areas results in gains on both language and reading tests, but the reader should bear in mind the limitations of tests which have already been pointed out. It is plausible to conclude that language gains following such programmes reflect a growth in confidence as much as in language competence and it is at this level that they are best interpreted. The confidence itself is likely to benefit a child's attitude to reading.

iii. Language and reading at reading age nine and above

At more advanced stages pupils have a wealth of language and, as we have pointed out in the previous chapter, in most classrooms they are given little chance to use it (Chapter 2, section iii). Theories of teaching which rely on both oral work and reading offer different suggestions for the most effective combination. At one extreme, formal language of any kind is dismissed as being unlikely to foster the involvement necessary for learning[12]. On the other hand researchers conclude that reading probably contributes considerably to the vocabulary and breadth of understanding of successful children[13].

The advantages of speech—the most direct communication medium—in arousing interest are obvious. But we have already referred to most teachers' lack of success in ensuring adequate pupil participation in class discussion. It is usually suggested that talk and experience should precede reading and this relates to ideas on the role of prediction in reading comprehension, which we examine in the next paragraph. The hope is that talk before reading will increase understanding of a text. However in accordance with the approach of two Schools Council projects[14] we suspect it is the inevitability of a mechanical written follow-up which inculcates in many children the habit of mechanical, uncomprehending reading. Although results have not yet been statistically analysed we are optimistic about experiments based on small-group discussion as a follow-up to reading study[15].

The mechanics of the reading process at this stage and the role played by preceding language experience are still the subject of debate. In many quarters the ability to predict meanings and outcomes in a reading passage is regarded as the single most important skill[16]. This is reflected in the current vogue for cloze testing. While prediction is important, and probably automatic in fluent reading in many contexts, the ability to decode, letter by letter where necessary, and digest the unexpected word or idea from print obviously plays an important part in effective learning, particularly where a teacher is not always at hand. While it seems unlikely that fluent readers call on these decoding skills in most of their reading, their importance cannot be ignored. While prediction of letters and grammatical sequences is likely to play an automatic part in efficient reading, attempts to teach it are highly questionable, and the emphasis of the cloze test may have unfortunate implications for teaching method. It is obvious that anybody trained to predict or guess the next word may not bother to read it accurately. Although the decoder who analysed fluent reading in terms of single letter recognition tended to overstate his case at a recent American conference[17] his paper offered a salutary reminder that there is more than one description of the reading process that is consistent with all existing evidence.

Notes to Chapter 3

1. Francis, 1975.
2. Latham, 1971 (Happy Venture).
3. For example, Thackray and Thackray, 1974. The manual shows that the tests have very low predictability for later reading ability.
4 For example, Belmont *et al.*, 1973; Bradley, 1955.
5 Stott, 1971a.
6 Spache formula. In Latham, 1971.
7 Example from Vernon, 1966. The difficulty in this test is weighed towards vocabulary rather than phonics.
8 Sigel *et al.*, 1966.
9 Moffett, 1968.
10. Olson, 1971.
11. Lawrence, 1971.
12. Rosen, 1973.
13. Clark, 1976.
14. Lunzer, 1976; Stenhouse, 1970.
15. Lunzer, 1976.
16. Smith, 1971.
17. Gough, in Kavanagh and Mattingly, 1972.

Chapter 4

Defining a Reading Problem

Summary

Research findings can be useful when teachers are deciding which children should qualify for special reading help and what sort of help they need. Generalized conclusions, however, may not always apply to local circumstances or to particular stages. Even in our compressed review we have to look at each school year separately. In the early stages the scheme used will influence the skills developed. Standardized tests are therefore likely to reflect the emphasis of the methods used until the end of the second year. There is little to be said in favour of waiting until a child is 'ready' before beginning to teach reading. Teachers should make sure poor readers actually get all the special help that they are reported to have.

In the secondary school more needs to be done for the children who, on entry, can hardly read or write. Structured methods with frequent limited goals are likely to be successful. For the next group, reading at an eight or nine year level, teachers must check the suitability of material they are asked to read. There is no research which establishes which type of school remedial organization is most effective, and there are good arguments to support several different models.

i. Introduction

When we admit the need to define a reading problem, we are assuming that solutions to the problem are somewhere available. Of course, problems are the products of circumstances and are unlikely to arise in classrooms where skilled and well-supported teachers have a chance to know each of their pupils well, to set suitable individual criteria for their work and to allow each to study subjects in an appropriate individual way. In schools today, where teachers are often expected to teach too many children too much too quickly, the teachers themselves have often not been trained to work with children who cannot read fluently.[1] Young teachers particularly are often dismayed at the prospect and are the first to ask how the research findings can help them to recognize and work with pupils who need special help of a particular kind in order to benefit from the general diet.

This is an area where there is plenty of useful evidence that is not generally acted upon. One sometimes sees, for example, an inclination towards an ill-conceived policy to exclude 'less intelligent' children (i.e. those with low measured IQ) from special reading programmes on the grounds that their reading difficulty is just part of general dullness. The research evidence on this point is clear; scores on intelligence tests give very little information about the ability to master the basic skills of reading.[2] In fact at the outset special reading programmes generally bring almost as much benefit to low-performing children as to their more successful counterparts in terms of gains on reading tests.[3]

In this chapter we suggest how teachers can most effectively observe their pupils, which points have been found critical in the path to literacy, and where a pupil's failure to reach such a point merits concern. We must, however, make it clear that research can only be useful to those who are aware of its limitations. We, for example, have been generally disappointed by the inconclusive results of experiments designed to predict which children will have serious reading problems. Children change so much over two years that even the best measures isolate only about 60 per cent of those who will have trouble, and this means that teachers should really watch everybody who is noticeably below average. Moreover the very word 'average' can only be defined in relation to a particular group. A child who is coping quite well with his reading in London could have a problem if he moved to Dumbarton.[4] In the same way most well-known and widely used reading tests set standards which are not equally appropriate across the country. Thus the Neale Analysis of Reading Ability was standardized in Birmingham and is known to over-estimate performance at the lower end of the scale, while the Southgate Group Reading Tests were standardized in Worcester where seven-year-olds seem to be six to nine months ahead of most others in the country.[5] The Neale is still a useful diagnostic test, and the Southgate can help to rank a group of children according to silent reading ability, but teachers must not take as gospel their estimate of national standards. We have not in this chapter included detailed discussion of reading tests. There is too much to say and it has already been well said elsewhere.[6]

We hope that the suggestions which follow will provide useful guidelines in conjunction with day-to-day observation and reasoned judgment. Research reveals unexpected trends which, minutely observed and truthfully recorded, can obviously give us new insights, but again we warn that neither a detailed case study nor a prototype from a large-scale survey will serve as an exact model for another real child. Even in this brief general summary we find it necessary to formulate different criteria for different age-groups. Moreover this chapter, which deals with recognizing reading difficulties, must be read in connection with the next, which investigates possible causes.

ii. Reading problems at infant level
Year 1

Some infants, as we said (Chapter 2), need practice in learning behaviour before they will learn to read. These individuals are not likely to escape the teacher's notice. Much less obvious is an unpromising pattern of learning ability. Since IQ is not a good predictor of reading success we must consider the skills which are. Some of these are rather surprising. Mostly they are not very closely linked with scores on IQ and verbal reasoning tests.

In a well-designed experiment[7] the ability to remember and reproduce a series of abstract shapes in the right order proved quite the best predictor of which children would read well two years later. This ability to retain order (or *sequence*) is a major factor in a number of activities which have been found to relate to later reading skill. Ability to match groups of letters,[8] to remember numbers in sequence,[9] to group pictures according to a previously shown or explained sequence,[7] and to spell simple words[10] can all be interpreted as indications that a five-year-old is going to be all right with reading. We shall mention sequencing again in the chapter concerned with teaching method.

Hearing and listening skills are usually reckoned as important to learning to read. The published experimental research about five-year-olds offers convincing evidence of three aural skills that are directly relevant. The most important is *blending*.[11] This involves the child listening to sounds (ee-t) and responding with the words they make. Promising readers will probably be able to combine five sounds given at two second intervals. Less promising five-year-olds will need a lot of practice to blend even three sounds. They will also have trouble in sound *discrimination*,[12] frequently mis-hearing, for example, *cap* for *cat* or vice versa. The third relevant listening skill involves hearing a sound or word and associating it with the appropriate shape or picture. Like reading itself it is an example of associative learning,[13] where abilities correlate highly with reading success.

Visually, trouble with the orientation[14] of shapes and letters (seeing and copying them upside-down or the wrong way round) is commonly associated with reading failure. Believers in dyslexia often quote this as an example of neurological malfunction, but experiments suggest it is a natural stage in learning to look and thus to read and write. With good teaching it will only persist in a very few cases. Many materials designed to help in this area test rather than teach. This will reinforce rather than eliminate the confusion.

Year 2

Most reading test scores reflect experience rather than ability among six-year-olds, who tend to do well on an exercise which is related to their reading scheme and badly on one that isn't. It is therefore difficult to compare standards between schools. Most teachers keep records of pupils' progress along a particular reading course. During the second year however pupils are expected to begin generalizing from their initial reading vocabulary. Those who fall behind at this stage are likely to need explicit help with the skills not emphasized in their scheme. There is evidence[15] that the less able will be particularly bad at word building and also that they will be among those who never pick up a book for information of pleasure. Whatever their method, therefore teachers should watch these points and be prepared to intervene with special teaching and encouragement where necessary.

The Bullock Committee noticed a tendency for poor readers to be given time with 'special' teachers rather than with the teacher they knew.[16] The report implies this is unfortunate, possibly for two reasons: communication between teachers is such that class teachers are not always aware of a child's special reading programme and cannot therefore reinforce it in the way we have suggested; the children who need the closest relationship with the class teacher are least likely to get it. We are not aware of the evidence behind this reasoning.

The Bullock survey gives an encouraging account of the amount of attention teachers expect to give their classes. Ninety-eight per cent of the poorest readers are expected to read individually to the teacher at least three or four times a week, and three-quarters of them get some sort of special attention in a small group. Experience, however leads us to be wary of these findings. In practice, absenteeism or school functions often interrupt the individual reading aloud; and the 'special reading group' tends to be the first casualty when staff are absent. Other figures from the survey present a more recognizable picture— nearly half the infant schools tested the six-year-olds but did not follow up the tests with specially prescribed programmes; and (unless the survey sample was surprisingly biased), some teachers must have overestimated their pupils' reading ability to quite a worrying extent.

By the end of infant schooling, standardized reading tests give a reliable estimate of reading prowess. This means that group screening tests are relevant at seven plus.[16] There is not much point in these unless the children who are considered at risk (generally about the lowest 30 per cent of an LEA population) are then looked at in much greater detail.[17] Observations of teachers and parents and consultation with social workers and doctors are important at this stage. Individualized remedial programmes based on simple diagnostic tests can then be implemented.

iii Reading problems in the junior school
Year 1

It is a likely though sobering possibility that 20 per cent of the children entering junior school will still be on Book 1 of their reading scheme.[18] This is a bad start to a critical year. We have already shown (Chapter 3) how reading vocabulary is expected to develop in seven- to eight-year-olds. This makes obvious demands on language comprehension. But the child who understands all the words is still not going to be able to read them without the necessary mechanical skills. From the studies we can conclude that most seven-year-olds can decode regular three-letter words (big, red, bud etc.) that they have not seen before. An eight-year-old should manage new words with less common vowel values (as love, father, and so on), combined vowels (e.g. lean, bite, flour/four etc.), consonant digraphs (ph, ch, th, etc.) and two-consonant clusters (*cry, swim* etc.).[19] Looking at 5,000 common words with this in mind we find that (ignoring the fact that he will have been taught some of them already) the first year junior is likely to cope with 180 at the beginning of the year, and 2,000 at the end. We can also expect marked development in spelling and writing skills. From now on, then, children are realistically expected to learn from print and express themselves on paper, and those who can't begin to know the taste of failure.

So far, then, some norms have been established, but what about our reading problems? In Liverpool nearly a third of the boys were still reading below a seven year level at the end of their first year,[20] while in Brighton[21] it was a quarter. (In both areas girls did not do as badly.) Yet in Dumbarton,[4] a largely urban area which includes Clydebank, only 11 per cent of boys (17 per cent of girls) were left this far behind, in spite of the fact that the group as a whole could be considered socially linguistically disadvantaged. Everywhere poor readers failed to recognize and pronounce the digraphs and clusters and were bad at building words. These findings can be used as evidence that systematic teaching of mechanical skills can go a long way towards reducing reading problems at this stage.

But there will always be a remainder who need a bit of extra help—the dull, the neglected, the dyslexic will be jostling for a place in the special reading group. There are unlikely to be enough places and quite a lot of work has been done on who should qualify for them. Roughly we can summarize the research as follows:

> Dull juniors who are behind progress almost as fast as the bright ones if they are given special help.[3] They can certainly learn to read well enough to join in normal classwork.[4] It is therefore misguided to treat an eight-year-old's intelligence score as a measure of reading potential, i.e. to use the gap between a child's 'intelligence' and reading scores to indicate whether he needs special reading. Where this is done the reading group tends to consist of verbal, usually socially privileged, children being coached to a very high level, while those who are struggling to cope with the class work, often from less privileged homes, are more or less written off.

We have found a more practical way at this stage is to help all those who are 20 per cent behind their age group (or 15 per cent in a high achieving school or one with plenty of help). This does not of course mean that 20 per cent of the children will qualify.[22] Any remaining places can be allocated to children with higher reading scores who are considered particularly likely to benefit. There are, of course, a few highly intelligent children who are seriously under-functioning (perhaps one for every ten children who are 20 per cent backward). The practical advantages of this yardstick are:

1. *All* the weakest children automatically get special help;
2. Objective measures avoid selection being influenced by factors like behaviour which may affect a teacher's impression of a child's performance;
3. No child stays too long in the group. This both makes room for new inclusions and ensures that the class teacher does not delegate responsibility for the group to the remedial teacher. It

also takes account of the inference[2 3] that consolidation in the reading group (staying there after minimal reading levels have been reached) does not increase subsequent progress.

A rough but useful guide to this method of selection can be based on the simple ratios of reading quotients.[22] To save the reader the trouble of computation we illustrate how this may be done.

Table 1:
Suggested cut-off points for selecting a special reading group of first-year juniors. All children who are reading below the age listed in column 2 (or column 3 where provision is limited) should be included. Remaining places should be allocated on teacher recommendation.

I		II	III
Chronological age		Reading age 15% below average (RQ 85)	Reading age 20% below average (RQ 80)
Years	Months	Years	Years
7	0	6.0	5.6
7	3	6.2	5.8
7	6	6.4	6.0
7	9	6.6	6.2
8	0	6.8	6.4
8	3	7.0	6.6
8	6	7.2	6.8
8	9	7.4	7.0

Year 2

The 20-25 per cent of boys in Brighton who began their second year with a reading age below seven improved very little, whereas the proportion of girls doing as badly continued to decrease.

Looking at these figures in conjunction with the other surveys[24] we begin to see a picture where:

1. Achievement is much higher in areas where pupils have already been systematically taught for three years.

2. Children (particularly boys) who can't read when they become second year juniors have often learned other ways to 'get by'. They seem to accept their role as non-readers until the year before they are due to transfer to another school. At this stage many of them put on a spurt.

3. Eight- to nine-year-olds seem particularly dependent on teacher help and motivation in order to improve their reading. The large-scale surveys of this age group were done some time ago (Bullock nine-year-old survey refers to the next year group), but Morris found that more than half of the poor readers in the second year never read to the teacher.[18] Most of the rest read once a week. So perhaps the lack of progress is not surprising.

4. Class teachers at this stage assume that most of their pupils can read, and use reading as the basis of most of their independent learning activities. So the backward readers are rarely able to work on their own. This has serious consequences—our group are not given a chance to work successfully on their own at anything, and they often begin to behave disruptively, or to withdraw.

The evidence therefore leads us to conclude that second year juniors are particularly in need of special help and motivation, and particularly unlikely to get it. Table 1 above and Table 2 below include suggested cutting points for selecting the special reading group from the second year.

Year 3

Compared with six-year-olds, children aged nine to ten will be spending less time on imaginative language (poetry, drama) and more on topic work. The Bullock commentary makes the point that much topic work consists of copying.[16] This could disguise the differences between good and bad readers, and hide some basic needs.

Teachers of third-year junior classes should not be surprised to find and make provision for one or two pupils reading below a seven-year level. These children may not know all the names or the sounds of letters and will certainly be unfamiliar with more complex phonic elements.[19] This means that dictating words to them, letter by letter offers little help. Written work as well as reading material must be continuously presented to them at a different level from that generally used with this age group. They are unlikely to be cases where high expectation will automatically result in high achievement.[25]

The next group, those reading between the seven and eight and a half year levels, will have begun to settle into certain reading habits. Different tests reveal different types of problems. A low score might for example signify fast, inaccurate reading, slow accurate reading, or mechanically correct but uncomprehending reading. The teacher must begin to be aware of these characteristics and use the knowledge in selecting the remedial reading group. If the remedial teacher is necessarily preoccupied in teaching basic word-building to near beginners, certain children reading at an eight-year-old level should rely on general class teaching to extend their skills. Stimulating classwork and conversation will best arouse their interest in words and in books.

With this in mind, we amend our scale for selecting the 'special readers'. We suggest that the *reading quotient* qualifying for admission should be lower for older children. This means that the older junior school children reaching a reading age of 8.6 years will be discharged from 'remedial reading'.[22]

Table 2:
Suggested cut-off points for selecting remedial groups of 9- to 12-year-olds. Most children reading below the age listed in column 2 will need help with decoding skills. Remaining places to be allocated by teachers as before.

I			II
Chronological age			Cut-off point (reading age at which learner could be discharged from group)
	Years	*Months*	*Years*
Less than	9		see Table 1
	9	0	7.6
	9	3	7.7
	9	6	7.8
	9	9	7.9
	10	0	8.0
	10	3	8.1
	10	6	8.2
	10	9	8.3
	11	0	8.4
	11	3	8.4
	11	6	8.5
	11	9	8.6

At this stage, however, we probably begin to need more exceptions to the rule, for we should also consider a child's writing and spelling ability. Generally children will learn to write words correctly about a year after they can read them. But there are cases, sometimes of highly intelligent children, where this does not happen. Specific remedial attention can often help, and save these pupils the frustration they are bound to feel as they are asked for more extended written work, and given less other opportunities to express their ideas.

We have already mentioned (Chapter 3) the heavy vocabulary content of reading tests above the eight year level. This means that several children will stick between an eight and nine year reading level in their top two years in junior school, often blocked by cultural factors. This group will not qualify for remedial reading on the terms we have recommended. They are likely however to benefit from situations which stimulate inquiry and 'research' involving both the spoken and printed word. We assume that all possible provision is made within the classroom for individual or small-group learning situations of this kind.

Year 4

As you will have gathered, most published research has been carried out within the conventional infant/junior/secondary school structure. The 10- to 11-year-olds are therefore expecting to transfer to secondary school at the end of the year. This probably helps to motivate the very poor readers. Morris found they tend to gain a year in reading age during this last year, and boys begin to catch up on girls.[18]

Apart from this, we have included in the previous (year 3) section some information which the fourth year teacher might find useful. He too will find the odd pupil who can decipher only a few words and he too will need to discriminate between the children who are still acquiring word-attack skills, and those who are limited by not having heard or been exposed to the words and ideas they they meet in their books. One researcher[26] concluded that between the ages of eight and 12 reading vocabulary increased by 2,500 words each year, so it's not difficult to see how many children get out of their depth.

By the time they are 11 the few highly intelligent poor readers/bad writers begin to pose an increasing problem of an opposite kind. Teachers should be aware of the results of the DES inquiry[27] which recommended that these children should be regarded as having specific reading or spelling disabilities, likely to be related to one if not more of the factors listed in Chapter 5.

iv. Reading problems at secondary level

1st–3rd Years (11- to 13-year-olds)

There has recently been a lot of argument about published research into reading standards in secondary schools. In fact it was concern over a (probably inaccurate) report that reading standards declined between 1961 and 1971[28] that led to the setting up of the Bullock Committee. As the dust settles, certain points seem clearly to emerge.

1. In socially disadvantaged areas a decline in language score is likely to be measured during secondary schooling.[29]
2. More than three per cent of new secondary school entrants are likely to be reading at *less than* a seven-year level (i.e. to be able to read only 180 of the 5,000 common words we discussed on page *five* of this chapter.[30]
3. The majority of these very poor readers are likely to be inner city (slum) schools. In one inner city comprehensive we find seven per cent of the first year with reading ages of seven or less. In another, we find 25 second and third year pupils scoring at a six- and a half-year level on Schonell's spelling test.[31] These are only two of the available reports.
4. Very low reading and writing attainments cannot altogether be explained by the pupil's 'dullness', for some of these same children do quite well (often coming near average) on tests of non-verbal ability and vocabulary.[31]

By the time they reach secondary school children will have diverged even more in their reading performance (fast and inaccurate, slow and accurate, etc.) than the nine- to ten-year-olds about whom we originally made this point. Their behaviour patterns too (absenteeism, lack of concentration, even plodding hard work) will have become established to a point where they inevitably affect reading attainment. Research models, whether from case studies or stereotypes from larger surveys, will not serve to describe the individuals in 2C who are the teachers' concern. 'Erroll Palmer is Erroll Palmer—reading age 6.8. He's the class clown; has a tough time at home; shows all the symptoms of dyslexia; frankly it's unlikely anybody's going to be able to do much for his reading now. He's a nuisance. But not such a nuisance as Robert Savage—reading age 7.2. Robert has terrible fits of temper (frustration?); is abusive and violent in spite of his nice mother; funnily enough he's got these dyslexic symptoms too. But there's a hopelessly long waiting list for special schools so we'll keep them here and do what we can. Actually both boys have odd flashes of real understanding. There was a class discussion on the role of the Police the other day . . .' and so it goes on.

Before going further it is worth checking just what to expect in terms of reading skills from children performing at a seven-year level. All the predictive abilities (noted on page 46) are still likely to be causing trouble, and teachers unskilled in diagnosis are most aware of the orientation problem (seeing and copying letters and words upside-down or the wrong way round; b for d; was for saw, etc.) since so much recorded work from children of this age involves copying.[16] As we have already pointed out, this is a natural stage in learning to read and write. Teachers expect it from six-year-olds. It is unlikely to signify neuro-logical abnormalities.[32] By the same token the mechanical areas where the children need help will correspond to those listed on page 46. At this stage, however, we can expand the lower end of the analysis.[33] Older children will almost certainly recognize consonants whose names and sounds are clearly associated (b d j k p t v z) and those where there is some association (f l m n r s x), though the others (c g h q w y) are likely to need attention. Twelve-year-olds have probably almost given up expecting to decode the vowels (a e i o u) because their values vary so much. Five words—father dad leaps late dark—can begin to illustrate the sort of hopelessness that invades a child when he is asked to associate a sound with the letter 'a'. The *vowel digraphs*, the *consonant digraphs*, the *consonant clusters* (cf page 48) all follow as areas that need sorting out and teaching systematically to *anybody* who is at this level of learning to read. The 12-year-old won't want to use childish books but there are certainly some which present this material especially for older learners.[34] Let us not, therefore, be too dismayed by Erroll and Robert's 'dyslexic' symptoms.

Our two friends were also alike in their nuisance value. Let us again turn back, this time to the comment on eight- to nine-year-olds (page 51). 'Class teachers at this stage . . . use reading as the basis for most of their independent learning activities, so backward readers are rarely able to work on their own. This has serious consequences—our group are not given a chance to work successfully on their own at anything, and they often begin to behave disruptively or withdraw.' We the authors, are not the only remedial teachers who've noticed the popularity of mechanical arithmetic with this group.[35] God forbid that we give them whole days of mechanical arithmetic; but perhaps the pupils are trying to tell us something which we should remember. Low achievers thrive on small finite tasks where they earn lots of ticks. The huge task of Learning to Read is too remote to mean anything to them—particularly when they know they've already failed in it.

We have some evidence that suggests these very poor readers are likely to feel fairly hopeless about life in general.[36] We must remember that only two or three per cent of the normal school population are achieving at quite such a low level. However we feel the severity of their problems justifies the amount of space we have devoted to them. The emotional and social aspects of their difficulties will be discussed in the next chapter. Before leaving this group we would stress again that there is no convincing evidence that older backward readers can reach a reading age of eight without systematic teaching of mechanical skills. This in itself is likely to build confidence.

Teachers feel that about 14 per cent of 12-year-olds in normal schools need special help. 10.4 per cent are getting some kind of help, but it is not at all clear whether the amount is adequate.[16] Most of either group are likely to be reading at an eight- to nine-year-old level, significantly above the children we have just been talking about. Equally, most of them are likely to come from less privileged homes. It is just at this eight to nine year level that vocabulary becomes an important factor in reading test scores. We have already mentioned relevant theories of language proficiency (Chapter 2) and related them to reading (Chapter 3).

Teachers who are working successfully with these children, either in mixed ability classes or in specialist remedial groups, will also simplify the material offered and make sure of its relevance rather than attempt to prepare the pupils to understand standard learning jargon. We have already pointed out (Chapter 2) how in an overloaded aural situation children learn to repeat the teacher's sentence accurately without attempting to understand it. They will also answer every written question by copying the book sentence that seems appropriate. They will have lost or failed to acquire the habit of finding interesting information from the printed word, and will use it purely to get the necessary ticks on their exercise to avoid being further bothered by the teacher. For many children the strategy is successful nearly all the time. If they are neat and careful they will probably not even be among the 13 per cent whose special needs teachers recognize. We have already mentioned the Effective Use of Reading Project (Chapter 3) whose methods avoiding written follow-ups are hopeful in this context.

Little satisfactory work has been done on formulating criteria for 'suitable' reading material. The subject matter obviously affects the difficulty, but must be assessed subjectively in the light of the reader's experience. A subject such as coal-mining could be graded at a nine-year level in Yorkshire and a 14-year level in London. Of course all teachers know that suitable preparation—visits, discussion, model-making or drama—will perceptibly ease the difficulty of a reading assignment. In Chapter 6, we look at readability formulae, useful to remind a teacher of the mechanical problems he is asking his children to cope with. Materials packaged in folders or spattered with pictures and big print are often deceptive. When analysed the writing often proves to assume a 12-14 reading level. This is serious if a teacher does not check before offering such work to his class; they will approach it with high hopes and be even more dismayed at their inability to use it.

Individual needs will vary widely in a group of 12-year-olds at an eight-year level. It is important to know how accurately they can *write* before deciding how far they should qualify for special help. Where a child is reading confidently at an eight- to nine-year level but cannot express himself at all on paper it is quite permissible to concentrate on developing writing skill. The inherent auditory discrimination and blending practice (cf page 46) are bound to benefit his reading as well as the relevant associative learning.

There is no significant survey we can find which relates secondary reading standards to class organization. On the assumption that a 12-year-old, reading and writing at a nine-year level, would benefit from normal specialist teaching with a cross-section of his peer group, one would press for the remedial specialist to work as one of a team of specialists presenting integrated studies to a whole year group.[37] The advantages might include specially prepared reading assignments on relevant topics, hints to the teachers who assume too easily that their pupils have understood difficult concepts, and so on. However a very large survey in the States found that most teaching teams had not yet learned to make use of each other's expertise.[38] We were surprised to find that nearly a quarter of the 389 secondary schools in the Bullock Survey had no special provision for 12-year-old reading and language problems and felt they needed none. There is certainly evidence that they were under-estimating the children's potential and their needs. In Chapter 6 we point out the dangers of 'integrated' methods being adopted for their economic advantages. But we have come across no research which establishes whether remedial specialists work most effectively within their own departments or with children who are integrated into other departments for most of the time.

A small residential special school in Durham offers the best example of what should be expected from even the most severely disadvantaged 12-year-olds.[39] The average IQ is in the middle 50s, and more than a third of them have been diagnosed as maladjusted by a psychiatrist, yet when a group of 20 12-year-olds left recently the psychologist found they were achieving an average reading above eight years.

In this context it is relevant to mention Hebron's research.[40] Looking at more than 1,500 children in secondary modern schools she found a recurring pattern of abilities among poor readers. Her subjects were not the lowest three per cent, but were reading at eight- to nine-year levels. They were not bad at arithmetic or at practical work (reflecting spatial ability). They were independent, self confident and persevering. They were twice as likely to be boys as girls and they scored very badly on anything concerned with words, reading vocabulary etc. Now our Durham group learned to read largely in a Special Programme Room, where they operated their own machines and were responsible for their own pace and progress. Such a situation obviously exploits the independence and perseverance which Hebron says we can quite frequently expect in the remedial reading group. Quite apart from using a reading programme which makes positive virtues of their characteristics, we would add that these individuals in particular are likely to react against any lesson where, because of reading and writing limitations, they are not given adequate opportunities for independent learning.

Fourth–Sixth Years (14-16 years old)

The Bullock Survey finds 10.2 per cent of 14-year-olds need special help, and three-quarters of them are getting it.[16] Unfortunately the numbers are not dependent on any particular standard. Investigations have shown that all pupils in ordinary schools can be taught to read to a nine-year-old level (which only demands the vocabulary of an average six-year-old). With skilled and imaginative teaching the average reading age of 15-year-old 'remedials' can consistently reach 12 years.[41] If such standards were suggested there might be a higher percentage of top secondary children diagnosed as under-achieving.

We are now, however, talking about young adults. The world of work dominates their thinking. If they can read well enough to take over a family market stall they are unlikely to try and do any better. On the other hand the army's success with 'illiterate' recruits shows what can be done if getting the right job is the motivating force.[42] There is one very interesting finding which affects this group. Most non-readers who learn to read as adults feel that they have done it by themselves—and could have done it before if they'd decided to.[43] They are appreciative of tuition—which has often been individual—but they do not consider it the main factor. There is surely a relationship between this, Hebron's independence finding and the need for individual, now work-oriented, programmes.

There are few investigations concerned with this age group, which might in itself be significant. Perhaps teachers feel it's too late to do much about them. Perhaps they are not at school very often anyway and therefore exempt themselves from the terms of reference of this review.

Notes to Chapter 4

1. DES, 1971; Headley, 1976.
2. Cane and Smithers, 1971.
3. Cashdan *et al.*, 1971.
4. Clark, 1970.
5. Moseley, 1975a.
6. Pumfrey, 1976; Vincent and Cresswell, 1976.
7. Hirshoren, 1969.
8. de Hirsch *et al.*, 1966.
9. Hirst, 1970.
10. Russell, 1943.
11. Chall *et al.*, 1963; Farmer *et al.* 1976.
12. Dykstra, 1966.
13. R. Evans, 1972; Muehl and Kremenak, 1966.
14. Weiner *et al.*, 1965.
15. Most of the skills we have just mentioned are obviously related to word-building.
16. DES, 1975.
17. Moseley, 1976; Wolfendale and Bryans, 1972.
18. Morris, 1966.
19. Carver, 1970; Davies and Williams, 1975.
20. Crawford, 1968.
21. Hammond, 1967.
22. Reading quotations $\frac{\text{reading age} \times 100}{\text{chronological age}}$ should not be confused with standardized scores. We are not seeking to pick out exactly the same proportion of children from each age group (see Table 2).
23. Collins, 1961; Moseley, 1975.
24. Clark, 1970; Hammond, 1967; Morris, 1966.
25. The unreplicated findings of Rosenthal and Jacobson (1968) seem more widely accepted than they warrant.
26. Gates *et al.*, 1938.
27. DES, 1972.
28. Start and Wells, 1972.
29. Halsey, 1972.
30. Sampson and Pumfrey, 1970; Start and Wells, 1972.

31. Moseley, 1975a.
32. Mattis *et al.*, 1975.
33. Jones, 1965; C. Moseley, 1970; D. Moseley, 1970.
34. Atkinson *et al.*, 1976; Centre for the Teaching of Reading, annually; SLA, 1973.
35. Blishen, 1955.
36. Gross, 1974.
37. For different views on this subject see Thompson *et al.*, 1974.
38. Olson, 1971.
39. Morgan, 1971.
40. Hebron, 1957.
41. Ablewhite, 1967.
42. Stevenson, 1972.
43. NARE, 1972.

Chapter 5

Factors Associated with Reading and Language Development

Summary

Conclusions from large-scale surveys are often based on correlations. A correlation implies only that two factors are likely to occur together, not that one causes the other. Failure to understand this has led to distortion of research findings.

Analysis of *regional and area* variations in language and reading scores establishes that the differences in achievement between areas within each region, although complex, are more significant than differences between whole regions.

Social class is the factor most closely associated with school failure. It is also linked to family size, overcrowding and certain parental attitudes.

Parental interest in education, however, is partly dependent on the attitude of the *schools* and this is likely to discourage working class parents. Teacher direction, quiet surroundings, and an actively involved head teacher are positively associated with achievement in reading. *Noise* probably has a more negative effect than has generally been recognized.

When it comes to considering *individual patterns* of abilities and behaviour related to attainment there is a danger that survey findings will lead teachers to expect certain general behaviour patterns in individual children. This must be avoided. There is no established evidence as to the nature of the association between behaviour and achievement. Poor readers are likely to show symptoms of poor concentration and restlessness. Depression, poor self-image and lack of confidence are also common among low achievers.

i. Introduction

When analysing research most of us find it very hard to remember that there is, as yet, absolutely no way of establishing that one set of circumstances causes another. Most misinterpretations—distortions—of research findings stem from readers who approach the subject from a particular viewpoint and then declare how statistics prove(!) that low achievement/vandalism/bad teacher-pupil relations are directly caused by comprehensive schools/structured language programmes/i.t.a.. These political publicists must be shown up for what they are, and we can only illustrate the weakness of their statistical understanding (depth of their statistical distortion) by giving a fairly detailed example of how a correlation does not establish a cause/effect relationship.

For this purpose we take a reported finding[1] that children from homes with only one (cold) water tap are likely to be behind with their reading. In unscrupulous hands this correlation could be used to support a wide variety of opinions, possibly including:

1. Parents who haven't managed better are likely to be of low ability; their children are likely, by heredity, to be equally ill-endowed.

2. Parents who are materially disadvantaged and also probably under stress, are unlikely to be above to give the children enough care and attention to maximize their learning capacity.

3. Children from such homes are likely to be in the least effective schools, to attend irregularly, and to suffer most acutely from the disparity between their own culture and that of the teacher. At best the teacher is likely to make wrong assumptions about their experiences—at worst she will approach them with low expectations or avoid them altogether because they smell.

4. Children from such homes are likely to be undernourished. Also they probably get their water through lead pipes which may well have adversely affected their brain functioning.

Now let us term these four explanations genetic, sociological educational and medical. Data from the same survey weaken the genetic argument in that a child's reading ability was not at all related to his *grandparents'* social position.[1] We are left with the claims of social worker, teacher and doctor. The social worker can quote evidence that reading ability increases when a child is given a chance to talk to a counsellor once a week.[2] The teacher can point to two schools who draw their pupils from very similar type of homes. In one school they all learn to read, in the other very few manage it.[3] The doctor can recall how de-leading therapy effectively improved the classroom behaviour of hyperactive children.[4] You can probably add to the list yourself from the often ignored and unsung small-scale work that goes on, with miraculous results, in every corner of the world. Offering the children breakfast,[5] getting them to cook bread in their own ovens,[6] having them draw up their own curriculum[7] might all be related to increases in both vocabulary and reading ability. Any kind of interest and attention seems able, *in certain conditions,* to lead to improved communication. But only painstaking and informed study will lead us nearer to knowing exactly what those conditions are. At the moment we have probably not even developed instruments which measure them. Before examining factors which have definitely been shown to be associated with developing reading and language skills, we take just two more paragraphs to underline the caution with which findings should be approached.

In the More Effective Schools programme[8] 12 schools more than doubled their expenditure per pupil for two years and yet the pupils showed no perceptible gains on a wide variety of measures including language and reading. Expenditure was more effective but results equally unexpected in another special programme.[9] For four years a team of one senior and two younger teachers were allocated to each of three groups of 16 children. The teams worked with three carefully devised curricula. Each curriculum emphasized quite a different aspect of work with four- to seven-year-olds: cognition, mechanical skills, or learning by play. Certain parts of the programme were common to the groups, the favourable teacher-pupil ratio, frequent home visiting, and, to judge from the film, the glamour of the staff. At the end of the four years all the experimental children had made large gains. But even on a battery of tests particularly designed to reflect the different emphasis of the curricula, there were no significant differences between the groups.

Now on the basis of these two results it would be possible to postulate that neither resources (money) nor curricular material was particularly related to achievement in schools. This would be an unpopular and unfair conclusion as most successful educational experiments have involved both. But we are in the position of the man with no chemistry set who always drank brandy and soda, and found he was beginning to lose his memory so he changed to whisky and soda, but it didn't help. Then rum and soda—equally no effect. Thus was he forced to the conclusion that it must be the soda. In our field, luckily, the results of most intervention seem to be positive. In the same way however we have as yet no instruments to measure which elements in any programme are those which actually have an effect on a child. Just when a major report[10] concluded that parental interest was the most relevant factor in scholastic success, we could have told you of at least two pupils who were doing badly largely because of too much pressure from home. And so far there seems no scientific or practical distinction between beneficial and harmful parental interest.

Only with such reservations firmly established do we dare to approach the subject of our chapter.

ii. Regional area differences

In spite of poverty, unemployment and old school buildings, children in Scotland and the North of England are less likely to be backward than those in Wales and the South.[1] The researcher who reported the Scottish superiority found six other differences between Scotland and England which we feel might play a part:

1. Scottish parents read to their children more regularly than English parents.
2. Scottish parents have higher educational aspirations for their children than English parents of equivalent socioeconomic status.
3. Scottish children settle down more quickly when they start school and fewer of them are unhappy there.
4. Scottish children speak more clearly than English children.
5. Scottish children attend school more regularly than English and Welsh children.
6. Systematic phonic instruction begins earlier in Scotland.

On the whole however, there are wider differences *within* the countries of the UK, and even within each city, than there are *between* them. Goodacre's London finding that reading scores are lowest in poor inner city areas and highest in the middle class suburbs is now widely accepted as being universally true and inevitable.[11] However, the relationship between poverty and low achievement in an area (home and family factors are discussed later) is not simple. There is now considerable evidence that there will be fewer bright children in a poor area, but not necessarily more backward ones.[12] Also, that from some poor neighbourhoods there come a number of girls who, at the age of ten, are achieving less than their seven-year-old scores would predict.[13] In fact, in Ireland 'deprived' Catholic children did as well as any when they were seven, but by the age of ten they were beginning to fall behind and sadly to match the sociologists' predictions.[13]

iii. Social and domestic surroundings

Examination of these findings leads us directly to social class and all its correlates. Nothing is more closely associated with reading failure. A seven-year-old with a manual worker father is three times more likely to be in the remedial reading group than his friend from social class 1, 2 or 3a.[1] This type of finding has been so widely publicized however, that before we spread it further we would add that half the seven-year-olds from social class 5 are likely to be average in reading and of these a third will be good, so there is no basis for having the Registrar-General prejudge a child's ability.

Socioeconomic status is associated with certain attitudes and conditions. Family size and overcrowding, parental initiative in education, father's interest in progress, and the literacy of the home are generally found to be factors which correlate with both socioeconomic status and educational achievement.[1] More than one study offers evidence that factors linked with social class relate more closely to reading failure as the children grow older.[14] Quotients tend slightly to drop among lower class children after the age of seven. Might they identify more closely with their parents? Or is it that morale and motivation wither as girls and boys become aware of difficulties at home and lack of encouragement at school? Again, there are many exceptions to the trend and we must beware of over-generalization, but a study in Northern Ireland[13] certainly suggests that in areas of high unemployment, working class children are likely to fall more behind with their reading as they get older.

The amount of time parents spend with their children and how they spend it have also been the subject of study. Good readers are likely to have had some help from their father at some time[15] although it is only among upper and middle class children that the absence of their natural father seems to be linked with backwardness in reading.[1] This fits with the theory that mother's education, not father's job best predicts a child's likely school progress.[16] Certainly children who read well are likely to have had a certain type of mother who could relate events to toys and stories the child knew, exploit the local facilities, parks, etc., give the child support in new ventures and approach his school with confidence.[17] Perhaps it is this type of mother who, left on her own, finds herself a job. This could account for the finding that children from one-parent families score slightly better where mother works than others from normal working class backgrounds.[18]

The relationship between home and school often emerges as a correlate of attainment. This too seems to be associated with social class. Schools in working class areas tend to see parents twice for every three visits in middle class areas. Moreover the working class schools hold fewer functions and those at times when fathers are unlikely to be able to attend.[10] However, this leads us directly on to the next section.

iv. Factors within the school

In situations where, as far as the human eye can judge, all other things are more or less equal, we still find some infant schools where everybody learns to read and others where they don't.[3] In Chapter 3 we pointed out that as reading ages advance beyond eight and nine years the tests are heavily weighted by cultural factors. Thus in the later years of primary and all of secondary education vocabulary and reading scores on standardized tests are unlikely to reflect apparent improvements in the classroom in response to short-term intervention. This is one of the reasons why much of the research is unsatisfactory, and helps to explain our emphasis on the early years.

The large-scale surveys[1 10 15] have established that socioeconomic status and parental interest are highly correlated with reading achievement. This matter seems more suitable for the previous section until we look in greater depth at the measures of parental interest. They involve visits, discussion, participation which are largely dependent on the attitude of the school. Encouragement is particularly necessary where parents might feel themselves to be culturally different from the teachers and where they are frightened of contact because they are aware that their child might be doing badly. Teachers who hesitate to take initiatives towards 'uninterested' parents should take heart from two survey findings: manual working class parents showed the strongest desire of any group to be told more about their children's progress, and were also the most likely to think that teachers should have sought more information from them about special problems and difficulties.[10] Moreover almost all parents however poor or in whatever trouble, welcome opportunities to talk to a teacher about reading and language.[19] When teachers knock on doors they can help to build up a sense of common purpose.

Most studies confirm that this is worth doing to improve achievement if nothing else. The Scottish data, for example, quoted at the beginning of the 'regional' section above are largely saying that the Scottish system succeeds because home and school support each other in progress towards mutually understood and agreed goals. When we look at the NFER's study of 10 infant schools[20] we find that in schools where achievement was lowest, all four teachers blamed parental lack of interest and 'extreme poverty of the children's cultural backgrounds' without specific evidence. These are the sort of accusations which deserve close examination, particularly in the light of the researchers' comment that the children were mostly well looked after and the standard of speech was 'better than one would expect for the area'. Certainly children's reading and language performance has significantly benefited from programmes designed to foster home-school contact.[21]

Theorists who are very much in favour of 'free development' could use the argument that parents do not understand and support their ideas to explain why their methods have been largely unsuccessful in teaching reading. Whatever the reason, the fact remains that when ten infant schools were studied in depth[20] the most successful differed from the least successful in the following ways:

1. Teachers exerted direct control over the children's learning without waiting for spontaneous or measured indications of 'reading readiness'.

2. Fewer classes were considered 'out of control'.

3. Early instruction in the sounds of letters was common.

4. The school sites were quiet (as opposed to those of the three least successful schools, one of which for example backed on to a railway shunting yard).

Points 1, 2 and 3 confirm some unpublished anecdotal evidence from an adviser who, over two years' study of a certain rather disorganized school, observed that certain children were most likely to learn to read during the term when there was a measles epidemic. Surprising gains were made by some of those who had three weeks at home where Mum, understanding her own goals, presumably offered direct control and systematic instruction.

Point 4, the noise finding, which was the most novel contribution of the study, is possibly more important than its position indicates. Instruction in letter sounds is almost impossible in certain rooms near a main road or airport. Moreover it has now been observed that, contrary to our expectation, children from ground and lower-level flats in tower blocks generally have more trouble with initial reading, particularly the auditory aspects, than those who live higher up.[22] Noise has also been found likely to affect concentration very severely in children with learning behaviour problems,[23] and it does not need research to underline its likely effect on the teacher. Perhaps seeming lack of organization was not entirely her fault. Pilot studies on the efficacy of learning through headphones[24] suggests it might be possible to ease the school situation immediately, though these can obviously offer only a superficial and temporary solution.

The influence of the head teacher is related to reading achievement in primary schools.[15] It is not surprising to find that heads get better results when they concern themselves in preparing clearly defined schemes of work and organizing special help for backward pupils. Of course the head also determines school organization, and it has been tentatively established[25] that where junior schools arrange a special smaller class for slower pupils, even if other classes are larger, achievements will benefit. Perhaps less easy to interpret are results (highly significant statistically) which show standards (in Northern Ireland) to be higher where the head encourages homework.[13]

Factors included in the NFER survey are as applicable to individual classes as to schools and are likely to correlate with differences in attainment. However there are no worthwhile comparative studies of matched classes with significantly different attainments. Although teachers' reluctance to participate can be well understood it is nonetheless regrettable. If it could be overcome, Goldstein[26] argues that new measures would be needed. Morris concluded that 'pupils attending schools with outstandingly good reading attainments had considerably better teachers each year than those in other schools', and her criteria for a better teacher included qualifications, experience and interest in teaching reading. It can be argued that the results justify the criteria. But Goldstein insists that more perceptive instruments for assessing teacher performance and classroom interaction must be developed if we are to begin to understand what makes a good teacher or a good school.

v. Individual personality and learning patterns

Large-scale studies of children's character are usually dependent on teacher or parent willingness to fill in questionnaires on every child. Small-scale studies show the limitations of this information and the dangers of over-generalizing from it. For example, outside observers have found teachers with unnecessarily negative attitudes towards slow learners[27] and gifted black children.[28] Now it is just possible that these are the teachers who, as students, learned that low reading scores correlated with antisocial behaviour[29] and colour.[30] Perhaps they are too inexperienced, too threatened, or just too busy to cope with, or even to perceive a situation which conflicts with a distorted impression from research that naughty children and black children are likely to have reading problems. When they come to filling in questionnaires on their pupils their observation and responses may be equally distorted and their wrong impressions become part of the next survey findings. One can see that the reputation of a certain group might be perpetuated by a teacher's expectation, as much as by what is actually happening.

To try and avoid such harm we want our readers to know that they are not likely to meet a pupil with all the traits we are going to discuss. The most interesting findings are tentative anyway. This section will probably be most useful if a teacher works out how many backward readers do *not* conform to the observed patterns. That way it might give a fairly balanced picture both of a group of children and of the applicability of the studies.

In Chapter 1 we discussed the evidence of twin studies and the likely part played by constitutional factors in determining attainments. However, positive intervention in certain cases has brought about amazing changes in achievement levels. You may have thought there was a printing error in Chapter 2 when we quoted the case of Terry whose IQ rose from 57 to 131 in six months. In fact he was part of an experiment group who achieved an average gain of 17 points over the six months.[13] Although large-scale surveys isolate certain groups as likely to achieve comparatively badly on tests relating to reading and language, smaller experiments convince us that physical or ethnic characteristics are a poor guide to a child's ability.[32] Teachers who achieve excellent results with so-called unpromising material, seem to be united in their energy and optimism, believing both in the children they work with and in their own ability to help them. They are undeterred by possible genetic limitations. Such teachers are rare and it is not surprising that pupils often revert to their former levels, when they pass on to a less stimulating and encouraging environment.[33]

Medically, positive correlations have been established between mother's smoking during pregnancy and baby's later backwardness in reading, baby's birthweight and later IQ, early development of eye-hand coordination and IQ, and late development of gross motor skills (crawling, walking) and IQ. A campaign against smoking during pregnancy is in operation, but we would not suggest trying to have a big baby, or stopping baby from pulling himself along the floor at an early age.

Investigations into the relationship between backwardness in reading and anti-social behaviour have produced no clear-cut results beyond the fact that a correlation exists. In an important Swedish survey Malmquist[34] looked at infant behaviour on entering school (aged nearly seven) and at behaviour and reading achievement at the end of the first year (average age seven years 10 months). When they came into school the subsequent poor readers showed a minimal tendency to be more nervous and to concentrate less than the group as a whole. By the end of the year, with reading problems becoming obvious, they were rated considerably worse on these behaviour characteristics whereas the normal readers had not deteriorated. These finding are probably reinforced by Stott's report[35] that rebellious attitudes and restlessness become increasingly common up to the age of nine—that is, during the critical period for acquiring reading skills.

However, before jumping to conclusions on the basis of these findings we should bear in mind that poor concentration and restlessness, as well as low reading achievement, are more common among children from social class 3b and below. And if we look at other useful surveys[36] we find that *fewer* backward readers are rated 'maladjusted' in schools with generally lower reading achievements. This suggests a variety of possibilities. For example, the norms of behaviour might be different in low-achieving schools; or non-reader might be a nuisance *per se* in a class where everybody else can read.

We have spent enough space on the difficulties of interpreting correlations, so now we merely state that we can find *no* statistical justification for a widely publicized conclusion that reading failure precedes truancy.[37] Certainly poor readers are likely to be bad attenders, but we cannot find figures which tell us which comes first. However an interesting light is shed by a small study of a secondary remedial department.[38] There was a highly significant association between truancy and lack of friends. This leads us to the depression and poor self image which have so often figured in studies of poor readers, and are equally found to be a barrier in language development.

The cheerful ignoramus features not at all in the research literature. Depression, low academic self concept, self-reproach, guilt, inadequacy and small hope of success are the order of the day.[39] Perhaps this is not surprising when related to other findings—the negative attitude of primary teachers to pupils who later turned up in the secondary school remedial department;[27] the unhelpful comments that one primary teacher offered to her low-achieving pupils while pupil-teacher interaction was being recorded.[27] Without suggesting a cause-effect association, we add to those observations the report that in New York, only isolates among teenage blacks accept the teacher's language model; the majority depend on their peer group.[40] And some of the brightest of the group are the first to drop out or consciously try to do badly.[41]

To return to our poor readers, we find they rate confidence high among desirable attributes, and many of them cultivate it with little foundation.[42] We are encouraged that evidence of measurable adjustment gains accompanying improvement in reading[2] were confirmed by the results of six months' work with poor readers in their first year at a comprehensive school.[43] Here, gains in reading accompanied the child's willingness to admit his nervousness, while those who made little progress continued firmly to deny their need of help. Perhaps this is the first measurable step indicating a much quoted pattern that development of basic skills helps a child to adjust to a school situation.

The patterns of learning abilities correlating with reading achievement have been discussed in Chapter 4.

Notes to Chapter 5

1. Davie *et al.*, 1972
2. Lawrence, 1971
3 Sproule, 1975; generally supported by findings of Chaza *et al.*, 1975.
4. David *et al.*, 1975.
5. Boxall, 1973.
6. Clough, 1973.
7. School of Barbiana, 1970.
8. Fox, 1967.
9. Weikart, 1971.
10. DES, 1967.
11. Goodacre, 1967.
12. R. Evans, 1972.
13. Wilson, 1971.
14. DES, 1967; Peaker, 1971.
15. Morris, 1966.
16. Brandis, in Brandis and Henderson, 1970.
17. Hess, 1968.
18. Ferri, 1976.
19. Chazan *et al.*, 1975
20. Cane and Smithers, 1971
21. Stenner and Mueller, 1974.
22. Cohen *et al.*, 1973.
23. A conclusion consistent with findings of Goldman and Sanders, 1969. See also Mills, 1975.

24. This is based on teachers' observations in the West Riding and a personal communication from Dr J. Forrester.
25. Moseley, 1975a.
26. Goldstein, 1972.
27. Nash, 1973.
28. Rubowits and Maehr, 1973.
29. Rutter and Graham, in Rutter *et al.*, 1970.
30. Jensen, 1969.
31. Hamblin *et al.*, 1971.
32. Hamblin's experiments are a good example but one can also quote Morgan, 1971, and descriptions such as Kohl's 1972.
33. This can be observed from anecdotal evidence from, for example, Kohl and Mrs Pyrah and is to be expected in the light of follow-up studies of pre-school programmes.
34. Malmquist, 1958.
35. Scott, 1971(b).
36. Summarized in Moseley, 1975a.
37. Rutter *et al.*, 1970; Tyerman, 1968.
38. Ralphson, 1973.
39. Barnett, 1972; Crawford, 1968; Gregory, 1965; Morris, 1966.
40. Labov, 1966.
41. Miller, in Schreiber, 1964.
42. Gillam, 1974.
43. Gross, 1974.

Chapter 6

Resources Available for Language and Reading Programmes

Summary

Although there are statistics and research studies concerned with the availability and effectiveness of resources, conclusions drawn from them are among the least convincing.

From the published figures it is impossible to deduce how much *money* is available for a given project. The accounting system effectively obscures the cost-effectiveness of any innovation.

Teacher time is the most expensive commodity and could be exploited and allocated more carefully.

School *accommodation* for the low achievers is unlikely to be as satisfactory as a recent survey concludes.

Technological aids can make a valuable contribution when they are properly used but no study is detailed enough for the frequency of proper use to be assessed. A few imaginative programmes reveal the potential of audiovisual media but effectiveness of most films, tapes, etc., depends entirely on the teacher's introduction and follow-up methods.

Learning *games* are on the increase. Many demand a small group teaching situation that teachers probably find hard to organize.

The range of *printed material* is extensive, particularly beyond the beginning stages of language and reading development. Various specialized and annotated bibliographies are useful. There is still a minority of pupils for whom it is hard to find suitable books and papers.

The use of resources outside the school has not been properly researched. A few published accounts imply they are considerable. There is evidence that visits and community involvement must be related to a carefully planned curriculum if low-achievers are to benefit from them in any way that has so far been measured.

i. Introduction

Practitioners tend to look to research, particularly at a time when money is scarce, for guidance as to the resources available and how they can best be used. In this area published information needs to be approached with caution. Section ii of this chapter points out the limitations of published analysis of how much money is available and how it is spent. In research on classroom resources, such as teaching aids, evaluation is nearly always open to question because of inability accurately to describe teacher behaviour—a critical factor we have already discussed (Chapter 5). In the same way descriptive studies which list or describe materials relevant to certain situations or types of learner, cannot make allowance for users' personalities and are necessarily a poor substitute for first-hand trials; although few teachers can afford to do without them as the amount of material grows. Such reservations explain why many of the points made in this chapter are concerned more with shortcomings of published findings than with their relevance.

ii. Financial resources

In one seemingly successful compensatory programme costs per primary pupil have been doubled in the belief that participants will not need social, psychiatric, or remedial intervention when they transfer to normal school at age 10.[1] If such a belief is justified, savings will more than cover the extra educational cost.

We know of no other experiment which has been costed in these terms, but such a sensible economic approach might free money for remedial programmes. For example, broken glass in Glasgow schools cost £375,000 one year.[2] In Knowsley £33,000 was voted to cover the cost of security devices for schools.[3] If heads or education officers could show that their policies were designed to effect savings in these areas, surely they should get the benefit. As far as we can discern, current educational accounting is designed to frustrate attempts to discover how and where resources are effectively used.[4] In fact it seems likely that cover for absent teachers and the maintenance of vandalized buildings and equipment make the least effective establishments among the most expensive, and also among those most likely to be eligible for more resources to waste.[5] Moreover requests for capital expenditure which might help eradicate the causes for these high running costs, are rarely balanced against possible future savings. Heads and authorities deciding their policies might bear these economic factors in mind.

There are constructive alternatives to suggestions that 'sink' schools should just be allowed to run down until they shut. For example in schools where achievements are particularly low or expenditure particularly high, groups of teachers might be asked to suggest

and implement possible remedies with direct advisory or psychological service support, thus partially lessening the autonomy of the head.
However such schemes initially depend on some objective assessment
of an unsatisfactory situation.[6] Financial resources can only be ration-
ally deployed when relevant figures are available for perusal by the
people who allocate the money.

Economics may play a part in the enthusiasm for the policy that
children with special needs should be educated within the normal
school. In 1972-3 the cost of educating each pupil for one hour was
13.6p up to the age of 11, 24.4p from 11-16, and 64.6p in a special
school. Individual attention was estimated at £2.50 per hour, and an
hour's attention in a group of six at 50p per pupil.[7] From these figures
we would argue that any head who now provides for children who
would have been in a special school is justified in claiming special
school resources. These could, for example, enable him to organize
plenty of attention for certain children, in groups no larger than six.
We leave our readers to consider whether the special resources are
likely to be maintained within the normal school without considerable
pressure from those directly concerned.

iii. Allocation of teacher time

Most of the costs just mentioned relate to teachers' salaries.
Teacher-time is the most expensive commodity in any educational
programme. Surveys investigating the allocation of teacher-time to
remedial readers come up with very varied results. Heads report that
nearly half the poorest readers aged nine are heard by a teacher every
day. Class teachers reckon to spend a total of about two hours' class-
time each week on reading. It is in fact probable that the person who
hears the poorest readers is not the class teacher.[8] Any remedial
teacher who has tried to withdraw her remedial readers in the second
half of the Christmas term, during the February staff 'flu epidemic', or
through the summer sports programme will know that daily meetings
are often easier in theory than in practice. The discrepancy between
time-table plans and achieved meetings whether in class or in withdrawal groups probably accounts for the fact that outside observers report
that the poorest readers aged nine are unlikely to have much chance to
read to a teacher. In fact one study showed that only one child in a
hundred was receiving 12 minutes or more individual attention a
week.[9]

Juxtaposing these two impressions (those of heads and of outside observers) leads us to recommend that heads, class teachers or remedial teachers might record the times when remedial groups are unable to meet if they want a fair picture of the time given to poor readers.

Of course the amount of teacher-time each child needs should to some extent depend on the quality of teaching offered. We have already mentioned how difficult it is to assess this. We find that about one primary school teacher in ten managed a short (six-session) course each year to learn about the teaching of reading. Fewer than one in 60 managed a longer course. At secondary level children of below average ability were the most likely to be taught English by people with no recognized English qualification. In fact, the 12-year-old remedial class was more likely to be taught English by a teacher in this category than by a teacher who had any special training in the subject.[8]

Bearing this in mind, we should perhaps not be too shocked to find that remedial classes spend nearly half their time copying, and much more than half of their English time studying language (probably in a mechanical way) rather than using it.[8] Again, with such information available, perhaps we should question the cost effectiveness of some of these teachers. Do these findings support Olson's observation-based idea that it would be better (because it is cheaper and at least equally educationally effective) to show a good film than to employ a supply teacher?[10]

Of course the long term answer lies in exploiting the teacher resource more effectively, and much energy is already being devoted to this end. Surveys have investigated the content of teacher-education courses and other examples of useful work in the areas of language and reading have been published.[11] One School of Education in particular springs to mind for its systematic and supportive work towards courses in language in colleges that fell under its auspices.[12] Now we are aware of findings that imply that teacher-control improves with the teacher's mastery of his subject.[13] But even so, we are dismayed by the fact that the teacher education courses all seem to concentrate on content of a language or reading course and fail to suggest ways of organizing the classroom. A major survey[8] did not even ask whether there had been any courses in departmental or classroom organization, and yet this skill is a basic requirement of any effective teacher deployment and of any effective language and reading programme. If you have ever attended lectures on really exciting methods or materials for language development you might have found, as we did, that only too often the honest lecturer admits that they are best used with a group no larger than six.[14] And when the teachers ask 'What do we do with the other nine, 24 or ??' the lecturer regards the question as beyond his subject. This point is of course related to the discussion of group size in Chapter 1, Section v.

Probably nobody knows exactly what leads or encourages a teacher to respond to individuals in the way that is most likely to result in their developing language. Thus training emphasis is placed on what makes good material for language work in the hope that once this is understood, the teacher will be able to organize accordingly. This does not follow, and therefore makes all the more welcome a course which gives explicit suggestions for classroom arrangement as an integral part of teaching method.[15] In the absence of relevant research findings we suspect that no theoretical grounding can establish the relevant organizational skills. If any methods are likely to be profitable, film or microteaching techniques are likely to play their part, and there are catalogues of audiovisual materials for teacher training.[16] However, viewing most of the films and videotapes intended to sensitize teachers to classroom language, one is disappointed to find that they largely fail to present language interaction at critical learning points. They tend instead to concentrate on a finished presentation or to depend on an overlaid (subjective) commentary to explain what is going on.[17] Neither can have much value. The advantages of a good working example, of training on the job by a competent experienced teacher begin to seem paramount.

Moreover the professional teachers—themselves on the front line— seem the body most concerned about the difficulties of classroom organization. It needs to be considered especially in connection with our low-reading-age groups. By definition these pupils tend to lack the key to most of the widely used independent learning situations. It was therefore particularly disappointing to find that the Bullock Committee did not see fit to include the National Association for Remedial Education among those 'concerned with the reading and the teaching of English'.[8] This association has produced some particularly helpful and practical information for teachers of the children we are writing about. It is one of their members, for example, who has produced a first-class clear analysis of various ways of arranging remedial classrooms.[18] It is under their banner that remedial provision was initially surveyed[19] and later teachers illustrated and discussed, for example, the pros and cons of different types of remedial organizations within

their different secondary schools.[20] Obviously NARE does not have
the monopoly of useful very practical information of this kind. We
look forward to the day when such detailed and applied thinking is
taken for granted as the day when teacher resources will be stretching
twice as far, and giving twice the satisfaction to pupil and teacher alike.

iv. Suitability of accommodation

From people we turn to accommodation. Generalizing from pre-
Bullock anecdotal evidence we had assumed that most remedial
reading groups met behind the stage, or in the broom cupboard.[21]
Again, the heads' answers confounded our impressions. Almost two
out of every three heads of secondary schools which had withdrawal
groups felt that these were suitably housed, while of the remainder two
out of five described the withdrawal accommodation as satisfactory
and only the rest (less than a quarter of the total) felt more could be
done.

Whenever a survey produces an answer like this, which conflicts
with a lot one sees and hears, there is always the likelihood that one's
own, unscientific evidence is atypical. However, we would also like to
point out in this case that the figures were produced by heads in
answer to a question which invited a positive response (Do they have
suitable accommodation?). Perhaps teachers who are more directly
involved would have shown less satisfaction. Perhaps heads would
have been more aware of shortcomings if 'suitability' had been more
precisely defined. Where language and reading problems are to be
effectively overcome there needs to be scope for all kinds of experiment and activity. Minimally one needs a sink, plenty of electric
sockets, plenty of room for wall displays, films, slides, a couple of
permanent tape recorder bases, and a permanent book collection at
least. We have no firm evidence with which to contradict the Bullock
finding. But since it is our job to present research critically we must
indicate that these figures could represent complacency rather than
justified satisfaction.

v. Technological aids

The Bullock survey also gives us the most recent information on the
spread of 'audiovisual hardware'.[8] Rather sadly in view of the excel-
lence of programmes for younger viewers, infant schools are the least
likely to use/have television. As the children get older the size of the
school seems to be a major determinant of the range of machines

available, and schools with fewer than 70 pupils can definitely consider themselves hard done by in this area. Of course the survey was investigating aids used in the teaching of English to all pupils but its findings seem a fair indication of their particular availability for low achievers. We were somewhat dismayed to see many more mains tape recorders were in use than battery/portable models. We also felt that the tables would have told us much more if they had also investigated the siting of the equipment and the use of headphones, loudspeakers and microphones. A departmental mains tape recorder carted into the average classroom cannot be considered a very high quality aid;[22] whereas individual or group learning from headphones attached to a permanently sited tape recorder offer a very desirable non-reader's alternative or supplement to print. In fact we see such equipment as an essential part of involving slow learners in mixed ability teaching.

The authors are committed to extending the use of technological aids.[23] Perhaps therefore we lay ourselves open to the accusation of saying sour grapes when we dismiss much of the published work on the subject as lacking in depth and application.[24] Like teachers, hardware resources can only be usefully assessed in terms of how effective they are. There are certain conditions which must be met before they can be said to earn their keep. We feel that many papers support the conclusions illustrated on film.[25]

1. Teachers must thoroughly familiarize themselves with one machine at a time. It is important to have opportunities to experiment with individual children and small groups outside the classroom before establishing the machine as an integral classroom resource.

2. It is necessary to master new techniques, and also, perhaps more important, to learn to be a classroom planner and evaluator rather than the instructor/supervisor teacher that conventional classrooms demand.

3. Repair/replacement services for all machines must be readily available.

4. Programmes must be easy to make or come by so that they can integrate well with other class activities.

5. Clear labelling, good storage and easy retrieval of programmes are vital. Under these conditions children have proved very responsible in looking after them.

6. Only two machines we know are self checking[26] to the extent of recycling the pupil each time he errs. Other work must be checked.

Sometimes the teacher can get feedback by discussing acquired information in larger groups; otherwise self-checking follow-up games and exercises can be prepared. One interesting study established that six- to seven-year-olds retained information from a language master better when they worked in pairs and checked each other than when they were checked by the teacher.[27] This is well worth bearing in mind.

7. There are children who cannot manage group work round a machine but will work all right on their own. These children should be allowed to work individually for some time before being asked to work with a friend.

8. Classroom aides should be available. The work needs teacher organization but groups or pairs of children often need adult help which can usually be adequately given by college students, older pupils, or other non-professionals.

Good teachers reading this list may feel that all this goes without saying—the fact that it is not always said perhaps helps to account for findings like that of the Individual Programmed Instruction programme in the States.[28] Here all pupils followed carefully prepared multimedia courses and the teacher's role was purely organizational. Under these the differential between the 'good' teachers (defined by pupils' mastery of subject information) and the 'bad' widened considerably as compared to their performance in a conventional classroom, i.e. the good teachers got better and the bad got worse.

Resource-based learning seems to be liked more by children of lower ability than by their cleverer friends.[29] Certainly teachers have noted increased concentration span when certain low achievers work in headphones.[30] Although this has not been analysed in a controlled experiment, suggested causes include the lack of distraction from other noise (already mentioned as a particular weakness of low achieving children, Chapter 5 page 67), and the privacy the child enjoys, knowing that he can replay anything he's missed, and that slowness or an unconventional response will not be immediately shown up in public.

The common tape recorder is the simplest and most versatile audio-aid. To see it exploited in a variety of ways paired with slide projectors, initiating children into skills both of language and manual dexterity, we recommend you to study the resources room at Dinsdale Park School.[31] The results here have already been referred to (Chapter 1, iii). This represents the ultimate and teachers must not be daunted if they cannot achieve the same degree of effective programming in their own situation. However, by any standards, so many tape recorders are badly or under-exploited in the classroom, that each case for more expensive and complex equipment must be considered, in these money-conscious times, in the light of how well it is likely to be used. If a teacher cannot make or be given time to get used to a new machine and the strengths and limitations of the machine are not well understood it may prove a white elephant. On the positive side, less common and more expensive machines have made a valuable contribution to education programmes for severely subnormal children, whose handicaps demand ingenious help. The Touch Tutor and the Possum Typewriter both provide profitable individual work at less than the cost of equivalent teacher help.[32] The Hansel Training Machine is less expensive and can recycle a learner who makes a mistake. Research has shown its appeal to be genuine (children like the novelty of any new machine and true value can only be studied when this has worn off) and also shown that after six months the children who work on it improve in independent learning capacity.[33] Although expenditure on such items may seem remote at present, the costs of educating children in special schools (section ii) suggest that the savings on integrating them into ordinary classrooms should make possible the purchase of worthwhile individual learning equipment.

Of course, as every teacher with a tape recorder knows, the machine is worth only as much as its programmes. 'Enrichment' is a term that effectively obscures/describes the objectives of many broadcast programmes, records, tapes and slides produced for low achievers and slow readers. The value of these depends on how successfully they are exploited and followed up by the teacher.[34] Materials which claim actually to teach specific reading and language skills must be looked at very closely. If a child is looking at an interesting book while he hears the story well read, the chances are that he is acquiring a positive attitude to reading and improving in word recognition. However for a hardened non-reader the materials certainly do not ensure reading improvement. We have seen children enjoying the tape story and not looking at the book. Equally, listening to the teacher's version of a language master card, then having the pupil record the same sentence or word, does not mean that the child is necessarily reading. Non-readers learn to get by without reading and again one of the authors has seen a child record a perfect set of language master cards with eyes tight shut in concentration so that he can listen, retain and record the words faultlessly. Admittedly these are the hardened cases. But if teachers are aware of them, materials can be found and designed to make such learners develop genuine reading strategies, and the benefits of such structured programmes for both teachers and low-achieving pupils are strongly indicated in a research study.[35]

At this stage it is appropriate to mention recorded materials designed to teach English to our non-English-speaking pupils. Until recently language-lab and tape materials seemed to depend largely on 'listen-and-repeat' exercises. These failed to take account of the learners' inability to hear suffixes and minimal differences between sounds undifferentiated in their mother tongue. Unless continuously monitored such exercises can only reinforce well-entrenched pronounciation difficulties and their only genuine contribution will be towards confidence. On the other hand, understanding spoken English, the basic skill, can be most successfully developed by presenting the learner with passages of gradually increasing length and complexity.[36] Actually producing speech once confidence is established, is best fostered by asking questions of another learner, recounting an incident or giving proof of having mastered certain information. For this, the situation is the programme. The material is an empty tape[37] or the ear of a native speaker. When it comes to teaching native speech intonation and pronounciation patterns, nothing is so effective as an interesting and attractive model (i.e. example). Since rhythm is so basic to English, the contribution of some language teaching records[38] must be mentioned. They offer a popular and effective stimulus for children from overseas. In this context it is relevant to note that there is now some research evidence that slower speech is more easily understood than quick speech.[39] This might seem to invalidate the swinging pace of the English recordings based on the prevalent counter-theory that it is important to learn to understand chunks of normal-speed English. It is not possible for the teacher to get the best of both worlds by playing the recordings slowly to start with, and increasing to proper speed as soon as the pupils get the gist of the meaning.

Since video recorders are becoming more common in schools it is worth referring to an interesting account[40] of how children were asked to describe themselves both in pictures and in words before and after viewing themselves on videotape. The complexity and accuracy of drawings and verbal descriptions increased, presumably as a result of watching the recording.

vi. Games

The activities we are describing all demand individual or small-group learning. They therefore lead naturally to a discussion of language and reading games. From the few studies we know it seems fair to conclude that any sort of dominoes, etc. will help to motivate the less able and develop some of the skills necessary for reading. Some good teachers have found that many games for low achievers are not a complete resource in themselves but are dependent on having extra manpower available.[41] The subject will arise again at the end of this chapter, when we consider resources available within the community. The number of different games available for reading and language development seems to be rapidly expanding at the moment. Some of these are fun even for children who do not need the activities involved. Often able and less able children enjoy playing these together. Other games are little more than competitive exercises.

vii. Other published material

There is now a vast amount of printed language teaching and reading material available for children performing below their chronological age. This is, of course, a good development as long as it does not encourage teachers to feel either that the material will do the work for them or that no further improvements are possible.

We have already mentioned the schism between approaches to mother-tongue mastery. It arises again here because the body of teachers who believe that language development must begin with Child Confronting Experience will be fundamentally opposed to any material or programme prepared especially for teaching mother tongue. The Peabody Language Development Kit (PLDK) is perhaps the best known and most extreme example of this category.[42] It comes in two orange tin mini-trunks at a cost of somewhere over £100. It contains, among other things, a puppet P. Mooney whose nose lights up when switched on, a P. Mooney bag from which the teacher produces various tricks, cards, objects, a P. Mooney xylophone on which he can play his songs, a variety of plastic fruit, a lot of flashcards and a very detailed teacher's book. It lays itself open to all the charges of bad taste, Americanism, and failure to allow the children to make their own spontaneous contribution or to explore their natural environment. It can be seen as the father of all structured language programmes which have been so bitterly ridiculed and attacked. Like most Aunt Sallies it deserves serious consideration and was found to have a positive effect after experimental use in four educational priority areas.[43]

Dr Smith of Peabody Institute was it progenitor. When he had responsibility for children's language in a large school area he was horrified by the shyness, the hung head and the turned-in toes of the six-year-olds going through the daily agony of 'news'—the spontaneous home-based utterances which usually comprised the main part of their language development routine. He grew even more dismayed as he realized that most of the mumblings he heard weren't 'news' anyway, but fiction dreamed up in attempts to meet teacher's expectations. For example, 'Mom took me to the supermarket and I stacked the goods in the car', and this from a kid whose family never owned a car anyway. So he produced the puppet who sang and lit up and wanted the kids to light up with him, who chanted all the common patterns of English and had the children do the same, until they grew confident in the classroom—eventually so confident that they held up their heads and said what they wanted to say. From another point of view, he produced a kit which forced teachers to organize their classrooms, a positive aspect of many structured programmes.

You can see it all happening on film[44] with a Bereiter programme. But be sure to watch to the end. Then decide whether for you the means are justified by the end, and if not opt for a gentler and probably less effective programme. Less effective that is, unless you are working with fewer than five children. For as we have already mentioned (page 17) less drastic situations can manage with less drastic solutions.

Psychologists have studied where children's language is likely to break down and have published ideas for helping to overcome these difficulties. Karnes[45] who has done such impressive work with preschoolers is perhaps the most thorough. There are also others who have made suggestions for improving memory, helping children to get things in the right order, to predict events in pictures and in words, to be precise about what they mean and to ask the right question.[46] Nobody goes to Peabody's length of supplying the plastic fruit—the most practical suggest utilizing rags and bricks and model cars, leaves and stones, all the paraphernalia of any lively young class. But where pictures are necessary teachers are probably most likely to use the schemes where they are ready provided.

We have already mentioned the opponents of such materials. However nobody would deny the advantages of access to a large and imaginatively stocked library whose resources ideally include books recorded on cassette,[47] filmstrips to accompany reading aloud to a group[48] and every kind of story and reference book to match the children's interests. The school librarian backed by the Borough Library Service, is probably the most powerful figure in most children's language development. They among others must also be given praise for the annotated bibliographies and reviews without which it would be possible to drown in the flood of new material.[49]

Apart from reasons mentioned in connection with Peabody, well-structured material is particularly welcome in teaching basic skills to low achievers in that it ensures that the children will not be expected to know something they have not been taught. Success is therefore more likely. Failure can more easily be diagnosed as inadequate teaching of something that has gone before.

After working with low achievers teachers tend to see books through their pupils' eyes. They then grow amazed, not at their pupils' failure but at how anybody learns to read at all. We find, for example, that key words are very often used in initial reading schemes with very little repetition although there is no mention in the scheme that they should be taught independently. We find amounts of supplementary materials, apparently basic to a reading scheme, being published anything up to ten years after the scheme has been launched in what seemed to be its final form. We find words in the text that are not listed in the vocabulary pages and which the pupils therefore meet quite unprepared. The number of new words in the early stages is in itself often a major stumbling block to a slow learner.[50]

Only in some of the most recent series has the skill of reading been broken down into a series of goals which seem possible to the older non-reader.[35] Moreover teachers have produced lists which link particular teaching points across the series. If for example, your pupil still gets in a muddle with 'a' and 'e', when he's finished the bits that should have taught him, you can easily find where the same point is made in a different book. That way, he need neither go on to something too difficult nor stick boringly on the same old page.[51]

Very few writers feel able to produce anything of much interest with a vocabulary under 300 words. It is only when a child is reading at a seven- or eight-year level, therefore, that he is able to approach the literature designed for slower readers. That is disappointing. However, considering that there was nothing at all in this category in 1946, we are encouraged to find nearly 100 series now listed.[52] In many of these serious attempts have been made to meet the attitudes and interests of the children who will read them. With this in mind it is surprising that so few of them illustrate or refer to black or brown-skinned English families.[53]

This leads directly to consideration of books especially prepared in children's speech dialects. Experiments in the USA have found that dialect modifications in reading material to match the children's speech do not significantly alter reading achievement. Where the children were learning to read traditional orthography, the speech pattern they used in school became nearer to standard English.[54]

Teachers selecting books for slow readers need to have some measure of what their pupils can manage. This is the purpose of readability criteria. The most useful we have found is produced by Mugford.[55] He has prepared a formula which gives each text a 'readability' age. It is based on the number of words in each sentence and the length of those words. Another good idea, if you have time to check each book with its intending reader, is to type out a short passage blocking out a word every so often. If the reader can make appropriate sense by filling the gaps, he'll manage the book. This method takes account of the effect a pupil's interest can have on his ability to cope with reading—but the practical results have not been found to differ more than six months from Mugford's assessment by formula.[56]

With the mastery of the basic skills reading ceases to be a subject in its own right and becomes a tool in general learning. A particularly useful study therefore looks at Schools Council project materials and analyses where and how they can be adapted to be used with children of limited reading ability.[57] This gives an effective lead in to the organization of lower achieving children in mixed ability learning groups. A similar approach could ruefully be applied to some of the imaginative English teaching materials from which less able children are excluded because they cannot read well enough.

viii. Resources within the community

The Educational Priority Area teams were among recent experimenters who tried to strengthen links between the school and the world outside.[58] In this they seem to have been largely influenced by sociological interpretation of the link between social class and school achievement. A paraphrase of their attitude could run 'children from working class homes tend to achieve badly. This is probably because the culture of the school is middle class and alien to working class children. If school and home culture can be brought nearer to each other, things will improve.' The nature of the possible 'improvement' varies according to the political position of the writer. Although everybody seems to feel the schools will be 'happier' places, as far as achievement goes, some want the measures to change so that they benefit different sub-cultural strengths—others expect the children to score better on existing measures. Whatever the outcome, these researchers are working only indirectly on improved performance. Their direct aim is to soften attitudes so that criteria can be mutually agreed and understood by school and community. The children are therefore likely to be better motivated and able to achieve well.

For our purpose here however we accept existing measures of achievement and look at elements outside the school which can be directly used to boost the low achievers.

Taking the categories of resource already used in this chapter, we start with money. The sum of voluntary contributions annually donated to slow learners or to schools in general has not as far as we know been established. There is always the danger that authorities would use it as a reason against taking statutory responsibility for certain areas of education. However, schools do have means of raising money, and seem to use them most effectively when they want to buy a particular item which will be put to good use. Since the slow learners' parents are likely to be the least able to contribute in this way it is particularly important that they should be well funded from other sources. Mr Morgan of Dinsdale Park acknowledges gifts from his local rotary club;[31] we know of machines for slow learners brought by Round Tables. Although they can be no compensation for inadequate authority funds, heads might bear these sources in mind.

Already we are talking about things rather than finance. Low achievers, as we've already mentioned, often have difficulty with abstraction. They often need direct experience with objects if they are to start talking about them meaningfully. So quite apart from means of learning such as machines or minibuses, the world outside schools has been found to provide material to learn from. The practice of asking pupils to bring from home 'old' things or objects relevant to a particular piece of work[59] is now apparently widespread and it is encouraging to find it has measurably positive results.[60] The American finding[60] that disadvantaged pupils produced their most complex language when discussing photographs they took at home of their favourite items is perhaps connected with the English tape/slide experiment[61] where low achieving pupils recorded technically precise and linguistically sophisticated commentaries to sets of slides they prepared on visits to places such as the local coal barge lock.

Of course hundreds of teachers are probably doing work like this and are too busy doing it to write it up as 'research'. Ablewhite was doing it all in the 40s but didn't get time to write it up until twenty years later.[62] Once a visit to the local iron foundry has become 'exploiting the Resources within the Community' perhaps Educational Research really has gone too far. But there is something to be learned from the written accounts. We see that each exercise was well structured with particular learning aims in mind, that the pupils had prepared defined active parts to play on their sorties. Deciding on a favourite object and photographing it was a very responsible task for an infant school child. Moreover the work was methodically followed up and eventually became part of wider projects. This is worth remembering in connection with the already quoted London EPA finding where a series of not inexpensive though much enjoyed trips resulted in slightly more decline in reading scores than that among children who just carried on in the classroom.[63]

Although we hear the local bargee on one of the West Riding EPA tapes[61] and we happen to know that some of the children got to know him well and learned a lot from him, there seem to be few written guidelines on how one can most effectively exploit the friendly people in the world outside school. Some of the Hackney ideas seem particularly hopeful—a local footballer putting his mark on a book written around local children; old age pensioners recording their reminiscences as a basis for history.[64]

Local people with more time and energy to spare can become regularly involved in the running of the school, and have been used as teachers' aides with particular groups of children.[65] There seems little methodical observation of different ways of organizing these volunteers—either in terms of their own satisfaction or of their effect on the pupils. Criscuolo[66] offers the most detailed account of parent participation in the classroom that we know but he gives no objective evaluation.

Student teachers are an equivocal resource as their first duty obviously lies in preparing themselves for work ahead. However there are accounts of projects where students have worked with individual slow learners and with small groups to the satisfaction of all parties.[67] Objective assessment of such experiments seems scant but a finding that the poorest readers learn most from young teachers[68] supports the view that these sort of enterprises have a particular value for the children with whom we are concerned.

Notes to Chapter 6

1. Stenner and Mueller, 1974.
2. TES, 1973.
3. Minutes of Knowsley Metropolitan Borough Council. £33,000 has been included in 1976-7 for the establishment of security patrols, the provision of various alarm systems, and certain building works to deter intruders. Included in this is a total of approximately £14,000 for a security patrol at seven schools.
4. Each year detailed breakdowns of educational expenditure are published by CIPFA (see references). When one comes to examine these, headings for actual expenditure one year do not match those of estimate for the next, and the classification of expenses on borough-wide bases (all teaching staff, all non-teaching staff, advisers' salaries presumably not included in training teachers etc.) makes it impossible to calculate how far considered capital outlay effects savings in running costs.
5. Otherwise known as 'payment by non-results'.
6. The government's recent allowances to EPA schools have obviously been devised with this in mind but do not adequately take account of the problems of schools with inefficient heads.
7. CIPFA, 1974; Hansard, 1973.
8. DES, 1975.
9. Morris, 1966.
10. Olson, 1971.
11. Buckley et al., 1975; CRC, 1970; Hannan et al., 1971.
12. University of Birmingham, 1971.
13. Flanders, 1965.
14. Other unsupervised groups can certainly be involved in similar work but experience in the West Riding (Moseley, 1972) and with Concept 7-9 (Wight et al., 1973) and Talk Reform methods (Gahagan, 1970) implies that the benefits are initially very small for the unsupervised children.
15. Levine et al., 1972 offer an example. Westwood, 1975, gives a useful analysis of different classroom layouts.
16. CELPIS, annually; C. Moseley, 1972; National Audio-visual Aids Library, annually. The Communication in Schools catalogue (Moseley, 1972) was devised to bridge the other two, one of which lists only college-produced material and the other only commercial productions.
17. The conclusions reached in this paragraph are based on a year's viewing of the material for the Communication in Schools catalogue (C. Moseley, 1972). While appreciating the technical difficulties of filming classroom language and the possible detrimental effects of showing imperfect practice, the benefits to students must be considered. There are exceptions to this gloomy picture. Some of the mixed material packages emerging from Colleges are useful. The already mentioned (Tough, 1976) Schools Council publication of videotapes to accompany a book is a valuable innovation.
18. Westwood, 1975.
19. Sampson, 1969.
20. Thompson et al., 1974.
21. We ourselves have worked in both these places. Perhaps a more common venue is the medical room—sometimes with a sick child groaning on the bed.
22. Speakers are needed for audible language reproduction in most normal classrooms.
23. D. Moseley, 1971a, 1971b; C. Moseley, 1970, 1972; Moseley and Sowter, 1972.

24. Useful accounts need to give details of the children involved, the classroom organization implemented, the programmes and follow-up devised and the work achieved.
25. Open University, 1973.
26. Hansel Training Machine and Talking Typewriter.
27. Hamblin, 1970.
28. Lindvall and Bolvin, 1967.
29. Alston and Hughes, 1976.
30. Teacher's observation in the West Riding, and personal communication from Dr J. Forrester.
31. Morgan, 1971.
32. Cleary et al., 1976.
33. D. Moseley, 1975b.
34. Ball and Bogatz, 1970.
35. Jones, 1965; McLeod and Atkinson, 1972; D. Moseley, 1971b; Remedial Supply Co., annually; Striker, 1977.
36. Wight et al., 1973; Listening Unit.
37. Martin et al., 1976; Smith, 1975.
38. Scope 1973; K. Wilson, 1971.
39. Daly et al., 1975.
40. Noble, 1975.
41. Smith, 1975.
42. Dunn et al., 1968.
43. Halsey, 1972.
44. Bereiter, 1968; Weikart, 1971.
45. Karnes, 1968, 1972.
46. Gahagan and Gahagan, 1970; Centre for Urban Educational Studies Language Division and ILEA Media Resources Centre, 1976; Shiach, 1972; for example.
47. An increasingly common practice, cf. Daly et al., 1975 for 1975 bibliography.
48. Weston Woods were the originators of this practice. Without it, many of the most beautifully illustrated children's books are unsuitable for reading to a group.
49. Atkinson et al., 1976; Centre for the Teaching of Reading, annually; Community Relations Commision, 1976; Day, 1971; Elkin, 1976; Hill, 1971; SLA, 1973.
50. Parker, 1971, 1973.
51. For example SMECC, 1976.
52. At the London Remedial Exhibition, 1976.
53. A bibliography with this in mind has been prepared in Haringey, HELRC, 1976.
54. Goodman, 1973.
55. Mugford, 1970, is straightforward to administer. Although not particularly scientifically devised it compares well with other formulae (Harrison, 1976).
56. Westwood and Fitton, 1973.
57. Gulliford and Widlake, 1975.
58. Halsey, 1972; Barnes, 1975; Midwinter, 1972; Smith, 1975.
59. Wood, 1975.
60. Cazden, 1970.
61. Smith, 1975.
62. Ablewhite, 1967.
63. Barnes, 1975.
64. Newton, 1973; Worpole and Boller, 1972; Worpole and Whitburn, 1972.
65. For example, Fryer, 1973; Nichols, 1974.
66. Criscuolo, 1973.
67. Buckley et al., 1975; Hannan et al., 1971; Otty, 1975.
68. Summers and Wolfe, 1975.

Chapter 7

Conclusion: The Allocation of Research Funds

Surveying recent major language and reading research projects in British is bound to lead to some general conclusion as to how well research money has been spent and to whether it might be better spent in future.

In the field of descriptive research, we have found Joyce Morris's survey of reading standards in Kent is a model.[1] Although her book is not primarily concerned to make recommendations, the detailed observations she presents tell their own story of what needs doing. One or two other British reports are equally useful in a more limited way while others have made little attempt to isolate factors which could help in assessing educational quality or designing improvement and some are unscientifically designed in the light of existing evidence. There is obviously need for a national body that can produce high standard work of this nature.

In the field of curriculum development the more limited projects seem the more successful. Teachers of children with overseas parents for example can find considerable support from materials specially produced from funded projects[2] but it is likely that no project has been generously enough funded to train many teachers fully to exploit the new ideas and kits. The recent move towards funding local projects to adapt and disseminate materials in conjunction with teachers' centres and local authorities is most welcome.[3]

Substantial funds have been spent both by Schools Council teams and by the Sociological Research Unit on more general questions of classroom language and reading. We have already commented on certain English teachers' unwillingness to present anything that could be related to mechanical teaching methods (Chapter 1, iii). This has led to some 'research' which rejects any reference to tests and objective measures. The reports emerge as a collection of anecdotes presenting children's work, sometimes of questionable value[4] without adequate details of the children who produced it. Classroom explorations of this nature are welcome in the sphere of private commercial publishing but hardly as the products of public research funds. At the other extreme the detailed linguistic and sociological analysis of the Sociological Research Unit reach such heights of theoretical complexity that teachers can see no possible application in most of their findings.[5]

The granting of curriculum development and assessment funds to universities rather than to local authorities may be a factor in the less satisfactory aspects of the work. In a crude paraphrase of what could go wrong, we suggest that research monies might be voted to academics as a result of urgent political pressure. Academics find that classrooms are not quite what they expected and recruit teachers. Thus some of the best practitioners leave the classroom. Attempting to generalize from limited experience to a national scale, they produce findings and materials which are too general to mean much; and before they can apply their work in different places, working with teachers, pupils and materials in a satisfying, applied and profitable way, the funds have run out. The political pressures are temporarily relieved, but other achievements are small.

All these difficulties are unlikely to arise where teachers, advisers, psychologists, researchers and statisticians work side by side, each in their own jobs, on a project with a defined local aim. The study that most nearly seems to meet this mode, apart from the work of some of the Educational Priority Area teams, is the Transition Assessment Study funded by the Social Science Research Council and the National Foundation for Educational Research (NFER), and carried out by the NFER in conjunction with the London Borough of Hillingdon. Here all concerned wanted to improve the quality of information accompanying children transferring from primary to secondary schools in the Borough. The project has resulted in assessment modules very similar to everyday assignment cards in the areas of language and number, which might themselves have a far-reaching effect on the junior curriculum. Cooperation between researcher and teacher at this level seems likely to generate the mutual respect and commitment which will result in a practical yet well-designed instrument. The project, although locally based, is unlikely to be without national significance.

Now we have heard, but cannot believe, that where subscriptions from many local authorities support a research body, none of the officers would be willing to see their subscriptions spent in a single rival borough. If this objection is genuine, it can surely be overcome by changing either the funding system, or the attitude to local projects— preferably both.

This review has attempted to bridge the gap between classroom and researcher. Direct funding would seem a more lasting and effective move in this direction.

Notes to Chapter 7

1. Morris, 1966.
2. SCOPE and Concept 7-9 materials were both the products of Schools Council teams.
3. The most recent Schools Council list of Projects includes eight such, based at Birmingham Structured Mathematics Centre, Bishop Lonsdale College of Education, Bulmershe College of Higher Education, Halesowen and Stourbridge Teachers' Centre, Madeley College of Education, Swindon Curriculum Study and Development Centre, Northumberland College of Education, University of Manchester School of Education.
4. The pupil's work quoted in Chapter 1, Note 4 would illustrate this point.
5. Bernstein, 1971, 1973, 1975; Brandis and Henderson, 1970; Cook-Gumperz, 1973.

References

ABLEWHITE, R.C. (1967). *The Slow Reader*. London: Heinemann.

ALSTON, R. and HUGHES, G. (1976). *An Anthology of Children's Comments on Resource-Based Learning*. Bristol: School of Education Research Unit.

ATKINSON, E.J., GAINS, G.W. and EDWARDS, R. (1976). *A to Z of Reading and Subject Books*. Stafford: NARE.

BALL, S. and BOGATZ, G.A. (1970). *The First Year of Sesame Street: An Evaluation*. Princeton, N.J.: Educational Testing Service.

BARNARD, B. (1976). *Reading Comprehension Test DE*. Slough: NFER.

BARNES, D., BRITTON, J. *et al.* (1969). *Language, the Learner and the School*. Harmondsworth: Penguin.

BARNES, J. (1975). *Educational Priority Vol. 3. Curriculum Innovation in London's EPAs*. London: HMSO.

BARNETT, B.R. (1972). Backwardness in reading, social adjustment and family attitudes. PhD Thesis, University of London.

BELL, J. (1976). *New Readers Start Here*. Oxford: The Library Association.

BELMONT, I., FLEGENHEIMER, M. and BIRCH, M. (1973). 'Comparison of perceptual training and reading instruction for poor beginning readers', *J. Learning Disabilities*, 6, 230-5.

BENNETT, N. (1976). *Teaching Styles and Pupil Progress*. London: Open Books.

BEREITER, C. (1968). *Language* (16mm film). Available from University of York Language Teaching Centre.

BEREITER, C. and ENGELMANN, S. (1966). *Teaching Disadvantaged Children in the Pre-school*. New York: Prentice Hall.

BERNSTEIN, B. (1971). *Class, Codes and Control Vol. 1*. London: Routledge & Kegan Paul.

BERNSTEIN, B. (Ed) (1973). *Class, Codes and Control Vol. 2*. London: Routledge & Kegan Paul.

BERNSTEIN, B. (Ed) (1975). *Class, Codes and Control Vol. 3*. London: Routledge & Kegan Paul.

BLANK, M. (1973). *Teaching Learning in the Pre-School*. Columbus, Ohio: Merrill.

BLANK, M. and SOLOMON, F. (1968). 'A tutorial language programme to develop abstract thinking in socially disadvantaged pre-school children', *Child Development*, **39**, 379-89.

BLISHEN, E. (1955). *Roaring Boys*. London: Panther.

BOEHM, A.E. (1967). *Boehm Test of Basic Concepts*. New York: The Psychological Corporation.

BOXALL, M. (1973). 'Multiple deprivation: an experiment in nurture', DECP Occ. Pub., 2, 91-113. London: British Psychological Society.

BRADLEY, B.E. (1955). 'An experimental study of the readiness approach to reading', *Elem. Sch. J.*, **56**, 62-7.

BRANDIS, W. and HENDERSON, D. (1970). *Social Class, Language and Communication*. London: Routledge & Kegan Paul.

BRIMER, M.A. and DUNN, L.H. (1962). *English Picture Vocabulary Tests*. Bristol: Education Evaluation Enterprises.

BRITTON, J. (1970). *Language and Learning*. London: Allen Lane.

BRITTON, J., BURGESS, T., MARTIN, N. et al. (1975). *The Development of Writing Abilities (11-18)*. London: Macmillan Education.

BROWN, R. (1973). *A First Language: The Early Stages*. London: George Allen and Unwin.

BUCKLEY, D.A., GILHAM, B.A., HAZON, J. and WATSON, G. (1975). 'Collaboration in reading development', *Remedial Education*, **10**, 3, 119-24.

CANE, B. and SMITHERS, J. (1971). *The Roots of Reading*. Slough: NFER.

CARROLL, H.C.M. (1972). 'The remedial teaching of reading: an evaluation', *Remedial Education*, **7**, 1, 10-5.

CARVER, C. (1970). *Word Recognition Test and Manual*. London: University of London Press.

CASHDAN, A., PUMFREY, P.D. and LUNZER, E.A. (1971). 'Children receiving remedial teaching in reading', *Educ. Res.*, **13**, 98-105.

CAZDEN, C. (1970). 'The neglected situation in child language research and education'. In: WILLIAMS, F. (Ed) *Language and Poverty*. Chicago: Markham.

CELPIS (1976). A Second List of Some Audio-Visual and Other Materials Made by Colleges and Departments of Education and Teachers' Centres. London: CET.

CENTRE FOR THE TEACHING OF READING (annually). *Books for Slow Learners*. Reading: University of Reading School of Education.

CENTRE FOR THE TEACHING OF READING (annually). *Reading Resources*. Reading: University of Reading School of Education.

CENTRE FOR THE TEACHING OF READING (annually). *Reading Schemes Suitable for 'Slower' Juniors 7-11 Years*. Reading: University of Reading School of Education.

CENTRE FOR URBAN EDUCATIONAL STUDIES LANGUAGE DIVISION and ILEA MEDIA RESOURCES CENTRE (1976). *Language for Learning*. London: Heinemann.

CHALL, J., ROSEWELL, F.G. and BLUMENTHAL, S.H. (1963). 'Auditory blending ability: a factor in success in beginning reading', *The Reading Teacher*, **17**, 11, 3-18.

CHAZAN, M., COX, T., JACKSON, A. et al., (1975). *Studies of Infant School Children 1. Deprivation and School Progress. 2. Deprivation and Development*. Oxford: Blackwell.

CHOMSKY, N. (1959). 'Review of Skinner's Verbal Behaviour', *Language*, **35**, 26-58.

CIPFA (annually). Education Statistics. London: Chartered Institute of Public Finance and Accountancy.

CLARK, M.M. (1970). *Reading Difficulties in Schools*. Harmondsworth: Penguin.

CLARK, M.M. (1976). *Young Fluent Readers: What Can They Teach Us?*

London: Heinemann Educational.

CLEARY; A., MAYES; T. and PACKHAM, D. (1976). *Educational Technology: Implications for Early and Special Education.* London: Wiley.

CLOUGH, P. (1973). 'Danilo Dolci: discovery at Partinico', *TES*, 23.11.

COHEN, S., GLASS, D.C. and SINGER, J.E. (1973). 'Apartment noise, auditory discrimination and reading ability', *J. Exp. Soc. Psychol.*, **9**, 407–22.

COLLINS, J.E. (1961). *The Effects of Remedial Education.* Edinburgh: Oliver and Boyd.

COMMUNITY RELATIONS COMMISSION (1970). *Education for a Multi-Cultural Society: Syllabuses.* London: CRC.

COMMUNITY RELATIONS COMMISSION (1974). *Education for a Multi-Cultural Society: Audio-Visual Aids for Teachers.* London: CRC.

COMMUNITY RELATIONS COMMISSION (1976). *Education for a Multi-Cultural Society: A Bibliography for Teachers.* (4th edn.) London: CRC.

COOK-GUMPERZ, J. (1973). *Social Control and Socialization: a Study of Class Differences in the Language of Maternal Control.* London: Routledge & Kegan Paul.

CRAWFORD, A. (1968). Unpublished study (mimeo). Abstract in *Bull. Brit. Psychol. Soc.*, **21**, 124.

CRISCUOLO, N.A. (1973). 'Ways to involve parents in expanding reading services to children', *Reading*, **7**, 11–4.

DALY, B., NEVILLE, M.H. and PUGH, A.K. (1975). *Reading While Listening: an Annotated Bibliography of Materials and Research.* Leeds: University of Leeds Institute of Education.

DAVID, O.J., CLARK, J., SVERD, J. *et al.* (1975). Lead and Hyperactivity. III—Behavioural Response to Chelation in the Hyperactive Syndrome (Preliminary Report). Mimeo.

DAVIE, R., BUTLER, N. and GOLDSTEIN, H. (1972). *From Birth to Seven.* London: Longman.

DAVIES, P. and WILLIAMS, P. (1975). *Aspects of Early Reading Growth.* Oxford: Blackwell.

DAY, A. (1971). 'The library in the multi-racial secondary school: A Caribbean book-list', *School Librarian*, **19**, 3. London: School Library Association.

De HIRSCH, K., JANSKY, J.J. and LANGFORD, W.S. (1966). *Predicted Reading Failure.* New York: Harper Row.

DEPARTMENT OF EDUCATION AND SCIENCE (1967). *Children and their Primary Schools.* (2 vols.) London: HMSO.

DEPARTMENT OF EDUCATION AND SCIENCE (1971). *Slow Learners in Secondary Schools.* (Education Survey 15). London: HMSO.

DEPARTMENT OF EDUCATION AND SCIENCE (1972). *Children with Specific Reading Difficulties.* (Report of the Advisory Committee on Handicapped Children). London: HMSO.

DEPARTMENT OF EDUCATION AND SCIENCE (1975). *A Language for Life.* (The Bullock Report). London: HMSO.

DOUGHTY, P., PEARCE, J. and THORNTON, G. (1972). *Exploring Language.* London: Arnold.

DUMONT, J.J. (1974). Research in programme evaluation. Paper presented at IFLD Conference, Amsterdam.

DUNN, L.M., HORTON, K.B. and SMITH, J.O. (1968). *Peabody language Development Kit.* Minnesota: American Guidance Service.

DYKSTRA, R. (1966). 'Auditory discrimination abilities and beginning reading achievement', *Reading Research Quarterly,* **1**, 5–34.

EDWARDS, R.P.A. and GIBBON, V. (1964). *Words Your Children Use.* London: Burke.

ELKIN, J. (1976). *Books for the Multi-Racial Classroom.* Birmingham: Youth Libraries Group.

ELLEY, W.B. and REID, N.A. (1971). *Progressive Achievement Tests: Listening Comprehension.* Wellington: New Zealand Council for Educational Research.

ELLIOTT, C.D. and PUMFREY, P.D. (1972). 'The effects of non-directive play therapy on some maladjusted boys', *Educ. Res.,* **14**, 157–61.

EVANS, A.J. (1972). Personal Communication to staff of Haringey Language Resource Centre.

EVANS, R. (1972). Swansea Evaluation Profiles: School Entrants. Technical Manual. (Report to Schools Council). Univ. Coll., Swansea. (Mimeo).

FARMER, A.R., NIXON, M. and WHITE, R.T. (1976). 'Sound blending and learning to read: an experimental investigation', *BJEP,* **46**, 155–63.

FERRI, E. (1976). *Growing up in a One-Parent Family: a Long-Term Study of Child Development.* Slough: NFER.

FLANDERS, N.A. (1965). *Teacher Influence, Pupil Attitudes and Achievement.* Washington: US Govt. Printing Office.

FLANDERS, N.A. (1970). *Analysing Teaching Behaviour.* Reading, Mass.: Addision Wesley.

FOSTER, R., GIDDAN, J.J. and START, J. (1972). *Assessment of Children's Language Comprehension.* Palo Alto, Calif.: Consulting Psychologists' Press Inc.

FOX, D.J. (1967). Expansion of the More Effective School Program. Centre for Urban Education. September. (Mimeo).

FRANCIS, H. (1975). 'Social background, speech and learning to read', *BJEP,* **44**, 3, 290–9.

FRYER, K. (1973). 'Parental Involvement Scheme', *Remedial Education,* **8**, 2, 35–6.

GAHAGAN, D.M. and GAHAGAN, G.A. (1970). *Talk Reform.* London: Routledge & Kegan Paul.

GATES, A.I., BOND, G.L. and RUSSELL, D.H. (1938). 'Relative meaning and pronunciation difficulties of the Thorndike 20,000 words', *J. Educ. Res.,* **32**, 161–7.

GILLAM, P. (1974). An Investigation into the Self-Concepts of First-year Secondary School Boys. London: Child Guidance Training Centre (mimeo).

GILLILAND, J. (1976). Improving Classroom Practice and Research. Address given at 1976 UKRA Conference.

GOLDMAN, R. and SANDERS, J.W. (1969). 'Cultural factors and hearing', *Exceptional Child*, **35**, 489–90.

GOLDSTEIN, H. (1972). 'Home and school. Plowden re-examined', *TES*, 55 May.

GOODACRE, E.J. (1967). *Reading in Infant Classes*. Slough: NFER.

GOODACRE, E.J. (1976). 'Reading research in Britain—1975', *Reading*, **10**, 4–10.

GOODMAN, K.S. with BUCK, C. (1973). 'Dialect barriers to reading comprehension revisited', *Reading Teacher*, **27**, 6–12.

GRAHAM, N.C. (1968). 'Short-term memory and syntactic structure in ESN children', *Language and Speech*, **2**.

GRAY, S.W. and KLAUS, R.A. (1970). 'The Early Training Project: a seventh-year report', *Child Development*, **41**, 909–24.

GREGORY, R.E. (1965). 'Unsettledness, maladjustment and reading failure: a village study', *Brit. J. Educ. Psychol.*, **35**, 63–8.

GROSS, J. (1974). Good and Poor Achievers in a Secondary School Remedial Reading Situation: A pilot study. London: Child Guidance Training Centre (mimeo).

GULLIFORD, R. and WIDLAKE, P. (1975). *Teaching Materials for Disadvantaged Children*. London: Evans/Methuen Educational.

HALSEY, A.H. (Ed) (1972). *Educational Priority Vol. 1. London: HMSO*.

HAMBLIN, F.A. (1970). Peer tutoring, token exchange effect on reading. PhD. thesis, University of St. Louis. (Summarized in HAMBLIN et al., 1971).

HAMBLIN, R.L., BUCKHOLDT, D., FERRITOR, E. et al. (1971). *The Humanization Processes: A Social Behavioural Analysis of Children's Problems*. New York: Wiley.

HAMMOND, D. (1967). 'Reading attainment in the primary schools of Brighton', *Educ. Res.*, **10**, 57–64.

HANNAN, C., SMYTH, P. and STEPHENSON, N. (1971). *Young Teachers and Reluctant Learners*. Harmondsworth: Penguin.

HANSARD (1973). Written answer to questions asked by Mr Parkinson, 25.10.73. London: HMSO.

HARINGEY READING CENTRE AND LANGUAGE RESOURCE CENTRE (1976). Multi-Racial Reading Schemes and Supplementary Readers at Primary Level. Haringey: Language Resource Centre (mimeo).

HARRISON, C. (1976). Investigating the readability of texts. Paper given at 1976 BERA Conference.

HAYNES, J.M. (1971). *Education Assessment of Immigrant Pupils*. Slough: NFER.

HEADLEY, J. (1976). 'Not trained to handle slow learners', *TES*, 16.1.76.

HEBB, D.O. (1955). 'Drives and the CNS (Conceptual Nervous System)', *Psychol. Rev.*, **62**, 248–54.

HEBRON, M.E. (1957). 'The mental and scholastic status of pupils in various streams of secondary modern schools', University of Hull Inst. of Ed., *Studies in Education*, **2**, 5, 400–19.

HESS, R.D. (1968). 'Maternal behaviour and the development of reading readiness in urban negro children'. In: DOUGLAS, M.P. (Ed) *Claremont Reading Conference, 32nd Yearbook*. Claremont: Claremont University Center.

HILL, J. (Ed) (1971). *Books for Children: The Homelands of Immigrants in Britain*. London: Institute of Race Relations.

HILSUM, S. and CANE, B.S. (1971). *The Teacher's Day*. Slough: NFER.

HIRSHOREN, A. (1969). 'A comparison of the predictive validity of the revised Stanford-Binet Intelligence Scale and the Illinois Test of Psycholinguistic Abilities', *Exceptional Children*, **35**, 517-21.

HIRST, W.B. (1970). Prediction of Reading Success. ERIC abstract of Amer. Educ. Res. Assoc. Conference, Minneapolis.

HUNT, J. McV. (1961). *Intelligence and Experience*. New York: Ronald Pres.

JACOBSON, L. and GREESON, L. (1972). 'Effects of systematic conceptual learning on the intellectual development of pre-school children from poverty backgrounds: a follow-up study', *Child Development*, **43**, 111-5.

JAMES, D. (1976). 'Rare bones (project at Lambeth Teachers' Centre)', *TES*, 15.11.76.

JENSEN, A.R. (1969). 'How much can we boost IQ and scholastic achievements', *Harvard Educational Review*, **39**, 1-123.

JOHNSON, D.F. and MIHAL, W.L. (1973). 'Performance of blacks and whites in computerised versus manual testing environments', *Amer. Psychol.*, **28**, 694-9.

JONES, A. and MULFORD, J. (1971). *Children Using Language*. London: Oxford University Press.

JONES, W.R. (1965). *Step up and Read*. London: University of London Press.

KAMIN, L.J. (1974). *The Science and Politics of IQ*. Potomac, Md.: Erlbaum.

KARNES, M.B. (1968). *Helping Young Children Develop Language Skills*. Arlington, Virginia: Council for Exceptional Children.

KARNES, M.B. (1972). *GOAL Program in Language Development*. Springfield, Mass.: Molton Bradley.

KARNES, M.B., TASKA, J.A. and HODGES, A.S. (1970). 'the effects of four programs of classroom intervention on the intellectual and language development of 4-year-old disadvantaged children', *Amer. J. Orthopsychiat.*, **40**, 1, 58-76.

KAVANAGH, J.F. and MATTINGLY, I.A. (1972). *Language by Ear and Eye: the Relationships between Speech and Reading*. Cambridge, Mass.: MIT Press.

KIRK, S.A., McCARTHY, J.J. and KIRK, W.D. (1968). *Illinois Test of Psycholinguistic Abilities*. Chicago, Ill.: Board of Trustees of the University of Illinois.

KOHL, H. (1972). *Thirty-six Children*. Harmondsworth: Penguin.

LABOV, W. (1966). *The Social Stratification of English in New York City*. Washington, D.C.: Center for Applied Linguistics.

LABOV, W. (1969). 'The Logic of Negro Non-Standard English'. Reprinted in WILLIAMS, F. (Ed) *Language and Poverty*. Chicago: Markham.

LABOV, W. (1970). Finding Out About Children's Language. HCTE paper 605 (mimeo).

LATHAM, D. (1971). *Six Reading Schemes: Their Emphasis and Interchangeability*. Cambridge: Institute of Education.

LAWRENCE, D. (1971). 'The effects of counselling on retarded readers', *Educ. Res.*, **13**, 119-24.

LAWRENCE, D. and BLAGG, N. (1974). 'Improved reading through self-initiated learning and counselling', *Remedial Education*, **9**, 61-3.

LEE, V. (1972). The Two Worlds. Open University radio programme E281/9. Milton Keynes: Open University Marketing Division.

LEVINE, J., HESTER, H. and SKIRROW, G. (1972). *Scope Stage 2 Teachers' Book*. London: Longman.

LIBRARY ASSOCIATION (1969). *The Reluctant Reader*. Available from County Libraries Group, Durham County Library.

LINDVALL, C.M. and BOLVIN, J.O. (1967). 'Programmed instruction in the schools: individually prescribed instruction', *66th Yearbook of Education*, 217-54. Chicago: National Society for the Study of Education.

LITTLE, A., and SMITH, G.A.N. (1971). *Strategies for Compensation: A Review of Educational Projects for the Socially Disadvantaged in the United States*. Paris: OECD.

LOBAN, R.D. (1966). *Problems in Oral English*. Champaign, Ill.: NCTE.

LUNZER, E.A. (1976). *The Effective Use of Reading*. Newsletter, Spring (mimeo).

LYNCH, J. and PIMLOTT, J. (1976). *Parents and Teachers*. Schools Council Research Studies Series. London: Macmillan.

McLEISH, J. and MARTIN, J. (1975). 'Verbal behaviour: a review and experimental analysis', *J. Gen. Psychol.*, **93**, 3-66.

McLEOD, J. and ATKINSON, J. (1972). *Domain Phonic Test Kit and Worksheets*. Edinburgh: Oliver and Boyd.

McNALLY, J. and MURRAY, N. (1962). *Key Words to Literacy*. London: The Schoolmaster Publishing Co.

MALMQUIST, E. (1958). *Factors Related to Reading Disabilities in the First Grade of the Elementary School*. Stockholm: Almquist and Wiksell.

MARSHALL, M.R. (1971). *Story Books for Retarded Readers*. Leeds: available from the editor, *The Yorkshire Librarian*, 28 Park Place, Leeds, LS1 2SY.

MARSHALL, M.R. (1975). *Each According to his Ability*. Oxford: School Library Association.

MARTIN, N., WILLIAMS, P., WILDING, J. *et al.* (1976). *Understanding Children Talking*. London: Penguin Education.

MATTIS, S., FRENCH, J.H. and RAPIN, I. (1975). 'Dyslexia in children and young adults: 3. Independent neuropsychological syndromes', *Child Neurol.*, **17**, 150-68.

MIDWINTER, E.(1972). *Priority Education: an Account of the Liverpool Project*. Harmondsworth: Penguin Education.

MILLS, J.H. (1975). 'Noise and children: a review of literature', *J. Acoust. Soc. Am.*, **58**, 767-79.

MOFFETT, J. (1968). *Teaching the Universe of Discourse*. Boston: Houghton Mifflin.

MORGAN, J.H. (1971). 'DIY at Dinsdale Park School', *Special Education*, **60**, 21-3.

MORRIS, J.M. (1966). *Standards and Progress in Reading*. Slough: NFER.

MORSE, W.C., CUTLER, R.L. and FINK, A.M. (1964). *Public School Classes for the Emotionally Handicapped: A Research Analysis*. Washington, D.C.: Council for Exceptional Children.

MOSELEY, C. (1970). An examination of the use of audio-visual teaching techniques for language enrichment among linguistically disadvantaged 11-13 year-olds. Dip. Applied Ed. Studies Thesis, University of York.

MOSELEY, C. (1972). *Communication in Schools*. York: Materials Development Unit.

MOSELEY, D.V. (1970). *English Colour Code Programmed Reading Course Manual*. London: Senlac.

MOSELEY, D.V. (1971a). 'A remedial programme for severely subnormal pupils with and without the Talking Typewriter'. In: PACKHAM, D., CLEARY, A. and MAYES, T. (Eds) *Aspects of Educational Technology V*. London: Pitman.

MOSELEY, D.V. (1971b). *The English Colour Code Programmed Reading Course*. London: Senlac.

MOSELEY, D.V. (1973). *Special Problems in Reading*. Option 5. Units 15-16. Open University Course PE261. Milton Keynes: Open University Press.

MOSELEY, D.V. (1975a). *Special Provision for Reading*. Slough: NFER.

MOSELEY, D.V. (1975b). Use of the Hansel Training Machine in Remedial Number Work. Paper given at IFLD Conference, Amsterdam.

MOSELEY, D.V. (1976). Folder material, Block 10, Course E.201. Milton Keynes: Open University.

MOSELEY, D.V. and SOWTER, D. (1972). 'The Hansel Training Machine: a new aid to (over) learning'. In: AUSTWICK, K. and HARRIS, N.D.C. (Eds) *Aspects of Educational Technology, VI*. London: Pitman.

MUEHL, S. and KREMENAK, S. (1966). 'Ability to match information within and between auditory and visual sense modalities and subsequent reading achievement', *J.Educ. Psychol.*, **57**, 230-9.

MUGFORD, L. (1970). 'A new way of predicting readability', *Reading*, **4**, 2, 31-5.

NAIDOO, S. (1972). *Specific Dyslexia*. London: Pitman.

NARE (1972). *Adult Illiteracy*. National Association for Remedial Education, 9 Cranleigh Rise, Eaton, Norwich.

NASH, R. (1973). *Classrooms Observed*. London: Routledge & Kegan Paul.

NATIONAL AUDIO-VISUAL AIDS LIBRARY (annually). *Film Library for Teacher Education Catalogue*. London: NAVAL.

NFER (1973). *Tests of Proficiency in English, Nos. 269-72*. Slough: NFER.

NEWTON, A. (1973). *Years of Change*. London: Centerprise.

NICHOL, H. (1974). 'Children with learning disabilities referred to psychiatrists: a follow-up study', *J. Learning Disabilities*, **7**, 118-22.

NICHOLS, R. (1974). 'Reading. I. Parents can help', *TES*, 24.5.74.
NOBLE, G. (1975). *Children in Front of a Small Screen*. London: Constable.

OLSON, M.N. (1971). 'Identifying quality in school classrooms: some problems and some answers', *MSSC Exchange*, **29**, 5. New York: Metrop. School Study Council, Inst. Admin. Res., Teachers' College.
OPEN UNIVERSITY (1972). *D100 08 Attitudes and Behaviour* (film). Milton Keynes: Open University Marketing Division.
OPEN UNIVERSITY (1973). *TV10 Course PE 261* (film). Milton Keynes Marketing Division.
OTTY, N. (1975). 'Getting it together', *TES*, 7.11.75.

PARKER, J.R. (1971). 'Success in early reading', *Remedial Education*, **6**, 3, 19–24.
PARKER, J.R. (1973). 'Reading Design 2: Some assumptions concerning basic schemes', *Remedial Education*, **8**, 2, 25–6.
PEAKER, G.F. (1971). *The Plowden Children Four Years Later*. Slough: NFER.
PINNINGTON, J. (1971). A Follow-up study of the children given remedial teaching in reading at the remedial teaching centre, Huyton. Dip.Tr.Diss., Edge Hill College of Education.
PUMFREY, P.D. (1975). 'The Illinois Test of Psycholinguistic Abilities in the diagnosis and remediation of reading failure'. In: MOYLE, D. (Ed) *Reading: What of the future?* 192–204. London: Ward Lock.
PUMFREY, P.D. (1976). *Reading Tests and Assessment Techniques*. London: Hodder and Stoughton.
PUMFREY, P.D. and ELLIOTT, C.D. (1970). 'Playtherapy, social adjustment and reading attainment', *Educ. Res.*, **12**, 183–93.

RALPHSON, H. (1973). 'Absenteeism in a remedial department', *Remedial Education*, **8**, 3, 29–32.
REED, N.C., RABE, E.F. and MANKINEN, M. (1968). 'Teaching reading to brain-damaged children: a review', *Reading Research Quarterly*, **1**, 289–98.
REID, J.F. (1972). 'Comprehension of syntactic features'. In: REID, J.F. (Ed) *Reading: Problems and Practices*. London: Ward Lock Educational.
REMEDIAL SUPPLY COMPANY (annually). *Catalogue of Learning Materials*. Wolverhampton: Remedial Supply Co.
REMEDIAL SUPPLY COMPANY (1972). *Picture/Language Scale*. Wolverhampton: Remedial Supply Co.
ROBINSON, W.P. and CREED, C.D. (1973). 'Perceptual and verbal discriminations of "elaborated" and "restricted" code users'. In: BERNSTEIN, B. (Ed) *Class, Codes and Control Vol. 2*. London: Routledge & Kegan Paul.
ROSEN, C. and ROSEN, H. (1973). *The Language of Primary School Children*. Harmondsworth: Penguin Education.
ROSENTHAL, R. and JACOBSON, L. (1968). *Pygmalion in the Classroom: Teacher Expectation and Pupils' Intellectual Development*. New York: Holt Rinehart and Winston.

RUBOWITS, P.C. and MAEHR, M.L. (1973). 'Pygmalion, black and white', *J.Pers.Soc. Psychol.*, **25**, 210–8.

RUSSELL, D.H. (1943). 'A diagnostic study of spelling readiness', *J.Educ. Res.*, **37**, 276–83.

RUTTER, M., TIZARD, J. and WHITMORE, K. (Eds) (1970). *Education, Health and Behaviour*. London: Longman.

SAMPSON, O. (1969). 'Remedial education services: report on an enquiry', *Remedial Education*, **4**, 3–8, 61–5.

SAMPSON, O.C. and PUMFREY, P.D. (1970). 'A study of remedial education in the secondary stage of schooling', *Remedial Education*, **5**, 102–11.

SCHOOL OF BARBIANA (1970). *Letter to a Teacher*. Harmondsworth: Penguin.

SLA (1973). *Books for Reluctant Readers in Secondary Schools*. Glasgow: SLA in Scotland.

SCHREIBER, D. (Ed) (1964). *The School Dropout*. Washington, D.C.: National Education Association.

SCOPE (1973). *Radio Camley* (Tape). Longman: London.

SCOTT, S. (1976). 'Dyslexia: a review of the literature', *Dyslexia Review*, **15**, 9–13.

SHIACH, G.M. (1972). *Teach Them to Speak*. London: Ward Lock.

SIGEL, I.E., ANDERSON, L.M. and SHAPIRO, H. (1966). 'Categorization behaviour of lower and middle class negro children: differences in dealing with representation of familiar objects', *Journal of Negro Education*, **35**, 218–29.

SIMONS, M. (1976). 'Collective wisdom—aims and work of the ILEA English Centre', *RES*, 17.9.

SKINNER, B.F. (1957). *Verbal Behaviour*. New York: Appleton-Century-Crofts.

SMECC (1976). *Supplementary Materials to English Colour Code*. London: Senlac.

SMITH, F. (1971). *Understanding Reading: A Psycholinguistic Analysis of Reading and Learning to Read*. London: Holt, Rinehart and Winston.

SMITH, G.A.N. (1975). *Educational Priority, Vol. 4 EPA The West Riding Project*. London: HMSO.

SPROULE, A. (1975. 'Of course we don't have any poor readers from you', *TES*, 21.11.

START, K.B. and WELLS, B.K. (1972). *The Trend of Reading Standards*. Slough: NFER.

STENHOUSE, L. (1970). *The Humanities Curriculum Project: An Introduction*. London: Heinemann.

STENNER, A.J. and MUELLER, S.G. (1974). 'A successful compensatory model', *Phi Delta Kappan*, **55**, 246–8.

STEVENSON, C. (1972). i.t.a. with Adult Backward Readers: A Survey of a Five-Year Experiment in the British Army. Evidence submitted to REHAB working party (mimeo).

STOTT, D.H. (1971a). *Flying Start Learning-to-Learn Manual*. Glasgow: Holmes McDougall.

STOTT, D.H. (1971b). *The Social Adjustment of Children*. Manual to the Bristol Social Adjustment Guides. London: University of London Press.

STRATTA, L., DIXON, J. and WILKINSON, A. (1973). *Patterns of Language*. London: Heinemann Educational Books.

STRIKER, C. (1977). 'Skills or interests?', *TES*, 14.1.77.

SUMMERS, A.A. and WOLFE, B.L. (1975). Which School Resources Help Learning? Efficiency and Equity in Philadelphia Public Schools. Business Review, February. Philadelphia: Federal Reserve Bank of Philadelphia.

THACKRAY, D.V. and THACKRAY, L. (1974). *Thackray Reading Readiness Profiles*. London: University of London Press.

THOMPSON, A., NEWTON, W., FLEMING, E.M. *et al.* (1974). 'Symposium on remedial education in secondary schools', *Remedial Education*, **9**, 9–21.

THORESON, C.E. (Ed) (1973). *Behaviour Modification in Education. Seventy-Second Yearbook of National Society for Study of Education, Part I*. Chicago, Ill.: University of Chicago Press.

TIMES EDUCATIONAL SUPPLEMENT(1973). '£375,000 for damage', *TES*, 9.3.

TIZARD, B. (1975). *Pre-School Education in Great Britain*. A report to SSRC. Slough: NFER.

TOUGH, J. (1976). *Listening to Children Talking*. London: Ward Lock/Drake Educational Associates.

TYERMAN, J. (1968). *Truancy*. London: University of London Press.

UNIVERSITY OF BIRMINGHAM SCHOOL OF EDUCATION (1971). Papers by members of the working party on the language component of the pre-scribed subject English for the BEd degree, 1971–2. Birmingham: School of Education.

VERNON, P.E. (1966). *Graded Word Reading Test*. London: University of London Press.

VINCENT, D. and CRESSWELL, M. (1976). *Reading Tests in the Classroom*. Slough: NFER.

WARD, J. (1976). 'Behaviour modification in education: an overview and a model for programme implementation', *Bull.Br.Psychol. Soc.*, **29**, 257–66.

WAUGH, R.P. (1975). 'The ITPA: ballast or bonanza for the school psychologist?', *J.School Psychol.*, **13**, 201–8.

WEIKART, D. (1971). *Early Childhood Special Education for Intellectually Subnormal and/or Culturally Different Children*. Ypsilanti, Mich.: High Scope Educational Research Foundation.

WEIKART, D. (1970). *This is the Way We Go To School*. (film). Available from British Film Institute.

WEINER, P.S. WEPMAN, J.M. and MORENCY, A.S. (1965). 'A test of visual discrimination', *Elementary School J.*, **65**, 330–7.

WESTWOOD, P. (1975). *The Remedial Teacher's Handbook*. Edinburgh: Oliver and Boyd.

WESTWOOD, P. and FITTON, S. (1973). 'Over to you: assessing readability', *Remedial Education*, **8**, 1, 35-8.

WHORF, B.L. (1958). *Language, Thought and Reality*. New York: Wiley.

WIDLAKE, P. (1972). 'Results of a reading drive', *Remedial Education*, **7**, 1, 16-9.

WIGHT, J., NORRIS, R. and WORSLEY, F.J. (1973). *Concept 7-9*. Leeds: E.J. Arnold.

WILSON, J.A. (1971). *Environment and Primary Education in Northern Ireland*. Belfast: NCER.

WILSON, K. (1971). *Mister Monday and Other Songs for the Teaching of English*. London: Longman.

WOLFENDALE, S. and BRYANS, T. (1972). 'Identification and follow-up of slow readers in the primary school', *AEP Journal*, **3**, 2, 77-80.

WOOD, A. (1975). Mosquito wings and milkmaids' yokes: parents as resource persons', *TES*, 2.2.75.

WORPOLE, K. and BOLLER, J. (1972). *Hackney Half-Term Adventure*. London: Centerprise.

WORPOLE, K. and WHITBURN, R. (1972). *If It Wasn't for the Houses In-Between*. London: Centerprise.

ZIGLER, E., ABELSON, W.D. and SEITZ, V. (1973). 'Motivational factors in the performance of economically disadvantaged children on the Peabody Picture Vocabulary Test', *Child Dev.*, **44**, 294-303.